SCIENCE AND INTERNATIONAL AFFAIRS
Melvyn B. Nathanson, *General Editor*

# It Seems
# I Am a Jew

## A Samizdat Essay
## by Grigori Freiman

Translated and edited
and with an Introduction by
MELVYN B. NATHANSON

Published in cooperation with
the Committee of Concerned Scientists

SOUTHERN ILLINOIS UNIVERSITY PRESS
Carbondale and Edwardsville

FEFFER & SIMONS, INC.
London and Amsterdam

Library of Congress Cataloging in Publication Data
Freiman, G   A
    It seems I am a Jew.

    (Science and international affairs)
      1. Freiman, G. A.   2. Jews in Russia—Biography.
3. Mathematicians—Russia—Biography.   4. Antisemitism—
Russia.   5. Scientists, Jewish—Russia.   I. Nathanson,
Melvyn B., 1944–   II. Title.   III. Series.
DS135.R95F68        947'.004924   [B]   80-404
ISBN 0-8093-0962-9

To the memory of my mother
SOPHIA MANSTEIN NATHANSON
1911–1973

# Contents

FOREWORD
    ix
INTRODUCTION, BY MELVYN B. NATHANSON
    xi
I. PREFACE
    3
II. STUDIES (IN THE PAST . . .)
    7
III. STUDIES (. . . AND IN THE PRESENT)
    17
IV. WORK
    31
V. SCIENCE
    38
APPENDIX A: THE SITUATION IN SOVIET
MATHEMATICS, BY EMIGRÉ SOVIET
MATHEMATICIANS
    85
APPENDIX B: "JEWISH PROBLEMS" IN
MATHEMATICS, BY MELVYN B. NATHANSON
    95
APPENDIX C: REMARKS ON "'JEWISH PROBLEMS' IN
MATHEMATICS," BY ANDREI SAKHAROV
    97

# Foreword

*In the vast and varied literature which deals with violation of human rights in the Soviet Union, Professor Freiman's essay is destined to occupy a special place.*

*First, the author, a noted mathematician, is neither a dissident nor a "refusenik." He is, as of this writing, still a Professor at Kalinin State University and a member of the Communist party (though perhaps not in good standing).*

*Second, the essay is not directed against the Soviet regime as such. It does not even attack Russian anti-Semitism. Except for the fact that it was legal under the Tsars and made illegal by the Soviet constitution, it has not changed in centuries.*

*The essay is about corruption of minds and souls of men, some of great ability and distinction, made possible by a blend of pathological anti-Semitism among a number of individuals and the uniquely Soviet scheme of rewards and punishments. Though of limited scope, for it deals only with mathematics and mathematicians, the essay constitutes, nevertheless, a powerful indictment of the Soviet system for providing fertile ground for the growth and spread of this corruption.*

*Freiman's amply documented J'accuse is mainly against a group of mathematicians at the Steklov Institute in Moscow who control much of the mathematical life in the Soviet Union. In particular, they control VAK, the certification commission which has the final say in approving doctoral dissertations. (A doctor's degree in the Soviet Union is much higher than our Ph.D. and it bestows upon the holder a number of privileges.) In recent years dissertations of excellent quality have been consistently turned down by VAK on flimsy, contrived grounds in the face of strong positive recommendations by acknowledged experts. The overwhelming majority of unsuccessful candidates are Jewish.*

*Freiman's own student (identified only as B in the essay) fell*

victim to this depraved system. *The magnitude of the corruption
faced by this student must have been what prompted Freiman to
expose the villains.*

Kafkaesque and Orwellian as the Freiman piece is, it is unfor-
tunately about existing reality. The offenders are not shadowy
ghosts but living, breathing beings whose names are finally being
brought to the attention of the world mathematical community.
For sins against truth and for rejection of the most elemental ten-
ets of civilized behavior, they have forfeited the right to be members of that community and for betrayal of noble principles of an
ancient discipline they shall reap shame.

Still, it must have been difficult for Freiman to write his essay.
We, on this side of the abyss, owe it to him to read it and to keep
it in our memory.

MAX E. GOTTESMAN
MARK KAC
*Cochairmen of the Committee
of Concerned Scientists*

# Introduction

## By MELVYN B. NATHANSON

Mathematics is like vodka. Drink, and you may forget the crude and oppressive world around you. Comrades and commissars, Komsomol meetings and Communist party propaganda, all fade away as you enter the pure and peaceful world of mathematics. Lie groups, algebraic number fields, partial differential equations, and other beautiful mathematical theories can provide a psychological refuge from anti-Semitism and other cruel facts of Soviet politics and culture. This escape into mathematics may be the secret of the extraordinary brilliance of mathematics in the USSR.

Mathematics is the best Soviet science. In all areas of pure and applied mathematics, Soviet scholars have obtained important and impressive results. Foreign observers sometimes claim that the reason for this success is the highly centralized administration of Soviet science, and, in particular, of mathematics. But Soviet mathematical triumphs have come about more in spite of this bureaucratic structure than because of it. Increasingly in the last decade, a vulgar politics has intruded itself into Soviet mathematical life. Jews have contributed disproportionately to Soviet mathematics, but now Soviet universities reject almost all Jewish applicants. Soviet authorities refuse to grant graduate degrees for dissertations by Jews. Editors of many Soviet mathematical journals will not publish research papers by Jews. Only one Jewish mathematician, Leonid Vital'evich Kantorovich, winner of the Nobel Prize in Economics in 1975, is a full member of the Soviet Academy of Sciences. Even Izrail' Moiseevich Gel'fand, one of the greatest mathematicians of this century, is only a corresponding member. The central institution in Russian mathematics is the Steklov Institute of Mathematics of the Soviet Academy of Sciences—the "Steklovka." The director of the Steklov Institute since its establishment in 1934 is Ivan Matveevich Vinogradov, a distinguished scholar and expert in analytic number theory, but also a passionate anti-Semite. The Steklovka employs over 140 mathematicians, but for many years only one Jew, Mark Aronovich Naimark. He died in 1978, and the Steklovka is now *Judenfrei*. Dissident, non-Jewish mathematicians also suffer. The distinguished algebraic geometer, Igor' Romanovich Shafarevich, a leader in the human rights movement in the Soviet Union and a member of the Russian Orthodox Church, lost his positions as Professor at Moscow State University and editor of the journal *Izvestiya Akademii Nauk SSSR* and has difficulty publishing his mathematical papers. It is a bizarre situation in the history of science.

Miraculously, mathematics has flourished. Like theoretical physics, mathematics is a science that you do in your head. You need only pencil, paper, and brains. Unlike biology and chemistry, mathematics does not require laboratories with expensive and sophisticated equipment controlled in the USSR by scientific administrators and party hacks. Pure mathematics can be done "unofficially" by workers officially employed in industrial establishments and in nonmathematical research institutes. If you have obtained at least an undergraduate education in mathematics at Moscow State University or at one of the few other good Soviet universities, then you can continue to do mathematics alone or with your friends.

Alas, political repression and increasingly virulent anti-Semitism have made even this unofficial participation in Soviet science difficult. Ten years ago, by doing extremely well on the entrance examination, brilliant young Jewish students might be admitted to Moscow State University. Now it is almost impossible, not only for Jews, but also for others whose background makes them politically suspect. It was once possible for Jewish mathematicians at least to publish their theorems in *Matematicheskii Sbornik* and other Soviet scientific journals. Now, under editor-in-chief Lev Semenovich Pontryagin, *Matematicheskii Sbornik* contains practically no articles by authors with Jewish surnames. Jewish scientists find it almost impossible now to find jobs in Soviet universities or research institutes.

The result, reminiscent of the exodus of scientists from Nazi Germany, is the emigration of large numbers of mathematicians out of the Soviet Union to the United States, Western Europe, and

Israel. This emigration includes scholars of the highest international distinction who have quickly obtained permanent professorships at Harvard, Yale, Cornell, and other American universities. Soviet mathematics is deteriorating. At Moscow State University, the Faculty of Mechanics and Mathematics has almost no Jewish students. It is ironic. In Tsarist Russia, where anti-Semitism was official policy, the government proclaimed a *numerus clausus* that restricted Jewish enrollment in universities to 3 percent. Today, in Communist Russia, where anti-Semitism is technically illegal, less than 1 percent of the mathematics students are Jewish. The Steklov Institute is *Judenfrei*. Parents are emigrating so that their children can get an education. Now it is almost impossible for Jewish mathematicians in the USSR to escape into mathematical research, to live independent of government scientific institutions, to work quietly at a dull job, and to prove theorems early in the morning or late at night. Soviet mathematics begins to reflect accurately the organization of Soviet science.

These remarks have a curious resonance in areas of public policy in the United States. Soviet practice in mathematics illustrates a general phenomenon. Apparently Soviet leaders have decided that they prefer dull but docile scientists to brilliant but politically unreliable ones. This may not be important now, but in the future it means that the USSR will have difficulty keeping up with the West in science and industry and will become increasingly dependent on imports of sophisticated technology. In the race for technological preeminence, Moscow will lose.

Grigori Abelevich Freiman is a witness to the distortion and demolition of mathematical life in the USSR. Freiman is Professor of Mathematics at Kalinin State University and the author of many books and research papers in number theory. He was born in 1926. In 1943, at age seventeen, he joined the Soviet Army and fought the Germans during World War II. At the end of the war, he entered Moscow State University and in 1949 received his undergraduate degree (in Russian, *diplom*). In 1956, he obtained the degree of Candidate of Sciences (*kandidat nauk*), which is roughly equivalent to an American Ph.D. In 1965, Freiman was awarded the degree Doctor of Sciences (*doktor nauk*), for which there is no

# Introduction

American equivalent, but which requires achievement in research far beyond what is necessary for a Ph.D. Freiman is also a member of the Communist party of the Soviet Union. This makes his essay, *It Seems I Am a Jew*, particularly remarkable.

Freiman's essay appeared in 1978 in the *samizdat* journal *Evrei v SSSR* (Jews in the USSR). Soviet censorship would never permit the publication of this essay. Instead, it circulated widely in *samizdat*. In Russian, *sam* means "self" and *izdat* means "publishing." *Samizdat* refers to the self-publishing of underground literature in Russia by means of the surreptitious distribution of many type-written copies of manuscripts. An American tourist in Moscow in 1978 acquired a copy of Freiman's essay and brought it back to the United States, where it was translated and circulated among American mathematicians.

Freiman has written a fascinating report on the difficulties that confront Jewish students and scholars in the USSR. To understand what Freiman is describing, it is helpful to review the Soviet system of education. Soviet children begin school at age seven. This is the eight-year school, which is divided into two four-year parts, elementary and secondary. Two additional years in a secondary polytechnical school are necessary for students who hope to go on to a university. There is a standard mathematics curriculum in all elementary and secondary schools in the USSR. At the end of the ten-year course, a pupil obtains the "certificate of maturity" (*attestat zrelosti*). This is required to apply for admission to a university, or more generally, to any institution of higher education (*vyshee uchebnoe zavedenie*, or VUZ). An applicant for admission to a VUZ is called an *abiturient*. To study mathematics at Moscow State University, the *abiturient* applies to the Faculty of Mechanics and Mathematics, or *Mekhmat*. There are four examinations in the admissions process: a written examination in mathematics, oral examinations in mathematics and physics, and a written examination in Russian composition. One of the current disgraces in this admissions procedure is a special list of extraordinarily difficult questions that are given only to Jewish applicants in order to exclude them "legitimately" from the university. Freiman gives a few examples of these "Jewish problems." A list of special Jewish problems in mathematics appears in Appendix B.

The undergraduate mathematics program at Moscow State University takes five years. The student receives a *diplom*, which is similar to a Master's degree from a good American university. Before he can apply to graduate school, the student must usually work for two or three years in a scientific research institute (*nauchno-issledovatel'skii institut*, or NII) or an industrial establishment to which he is assigned by the Ministry of Higher Education. Then he can become a graduate student (*aspirant*). The Academic Council (*ychenyi soviet*) of a university, however, can recommend that a student who has been approved by the local Communist party organization be admitted to graduate study immediately after obtaining his *diplom*. Most *aspirants* in Mekhmat at Moscow State University receive this recommendation and do not have to work in industry.

There are two stages in the process of obtaining graduate degrees in mathematics. First, one must defend a dissertation in a university or scientific research institute that is permitted to grant degrees in mathematics. Second, VAK must approve the degree. VAK is the Higher Certification Commission (*Vysshaya Attestatsionnaya Kommissiya*), a government body that must approve every degree of *kandidat nauk* or *doktor nauk* that is conferred in the Soviet Union. In each discipline, VAK establishes an Expert Committee to judge the quality of dissertations. For many years, VAK's Expert Committee in Mathematics has usually refused to recommend the award of graduate degrees to Jewish mathematicians whose dissertations had been successfully defended at the university level. Freiman describes how he struggled and failed to get VAK to confirm the degree of his own graduate student, a Jew, whose thesis had already led to the solution of an old and difficult problem in number theory.

Freiman's essay, "It Seems I Am a Jew," is a moving and beautifully written account of how Soviet science works.

This volume also contains three appendices. Appendix A is the *tamizdat* essay, "The Situation in Soviet Mathematics." In Russian,

*Introduction*

*tam* means "there" in the sense of "far away." *Tamizdat* refers to Russian literature published outside of Russia for readers inside Russia. The authors of "The Situation in Soviet Mathematics" are mathematicians who have emigrated from the USSR and now live in the United States and Israel. They cannot be named because of possible reprisals against relatives and friends who remain in the Soviet Union.

Appendix B is a list of the extraordinarily difficult problems in mathematics used to exclude Jewish applicants from Moscow State University in 1978. Appendix C contains a statement by the distinguished Soviet physicist and human rights activist Andrei Sakharov concerning these special "Jewish problems."

This book is being published in collaboration with the Committee of Concerned Scientists. I am grateful to Max E. Gottesman and Mark Kac, cochairmen of the Committee of Concerned Scientists, for their Foreword. I wish to thank two persons, one who brought the Freiman manuscript out of Russia, the other who quickly translated it into English, both of whom wish to remain anonymous. I am grateful to many Soviet friends in Moscow and America who have tutored me in the intricacies of Soviet life.

I discovered Freiman's essay at the West Coast Number Theory Conference in Santa Barbara, California, in December, 1978, where the manuscript was circulated. For this volume I have retranslated much of the essay from the Russian text.

This book tells a shocking story. It is a story about a few great mathematicians who are evil and about many lesser mathematicians who collaborate in evil acts to obtain good jobs, trips abroad, and other special privileges. For the sake of the mathematicians who still live in the Soviet Union, let us hope that those who corrupt scientific life in the USSR will soon lose their power and that their oppressive and anti-Semitic policies will cease.

# It Seems I Am a Jew

# I. Preface

## The Prince and the Pauper

This year, 1976, I will be fifty. Mathematics has always been the most important thing in my life. I studied it, enjoyed teaching it, organized research projects in it. When I finished one article, I immediately went on to a second. When I put the final period in one book, I began to think about the next.

And now the train, whose sole function has been to go "forward along the rails," suddenly stops. I no longer organize anything, and no one even asks me about it. I continue teaching out of inertia. Most important, I have lost interest in solving problems or proving theorems.

Why? Briefly, I am persecuted at my job because I am a Jew. My associates who are Jewish are also persecuted. Thus my enthusiasm for work has given way to gloomy meditation.

Is it worthwhile to continue? Do my personal troubles have any general interest?

Pondering this, I often converse with an imaginary critic. He runs up to me with a newspaper in his hand.

*Critic:* Are they persecuting you? Have they said to you, "Jew, get out!"?

*I:* No, they have not spoken so bluntly.

*Critic:* Everything is clear. It only seems so to you. But aren't the facts the important thing? So, you fought in the war after finishing secondary school?

*I:* In 1943, at seventeen.

*Critic:* After the war were you given the opportunity to study?

*I:* Your question is formulated in a strange way. Could it have been otherwise?

*Critic:* And you finished the university in 1950?

*I:* In 1949.

*Critic:* And seven years later you defended your Candidate of Sciences dissertation?[1]

*I:* Yes, in 1956.

*Critic:* And in 1965, the Doctor of Sciences dissertation?

*I:* Yes, but tell me, finally, what are you driving at?

In place of an answer, he unfolded his newspaper and read aloud:[2]

> I wish to declare in a loud voice: In our socialist country there has never been and there cannot be persecution of any nationality in general and of Jews in particular. The law guarantees equal rights to every citizen of our multinational country.
>
> My life can serve as an example of how Jews are "persecuted" in our country. After finishing secondary school I went to the front. After the war I was given the opportunity to study. In 1950 I finished the university and seven years later I defended my Candidate of Sciences dissertation, and in 1965 my Doctor of Sciences. Who can say that I have been "persecuted"?

I looked at the signature: V. S. Etlis, Doctor of Chemical Sciences and Professor.

I was swallowed up in thought. My troubles and anxieties were suddenly pulled into a furiously revolving whirlwind, which quickly left behind the hardness of the approved formulas of Dr. Etlis. The opposite poles of our opinions were galloping, leading us in different directions. I found myself in the forest of my life, where fireflies of memories twinkled in the night of oblivion and the familiar road of knowledge led to the horizon of the Problem. I set out along this road. The feelings of prejudice and partiality left me. Remember that some small piece of the approaching sun-truth also belongs to your opponent in the argument.

---

1. The Soviet degree Candidate of Sciences is roughly the same as an American Ph.D. The Doctor of Sciences degree requires considerable achievement in research beyond the Candidate of Sciences degree. There is no American equivalent.—Ed.

2. *Literaturnaya Gazeta*, 18 February 1976.

## On the Value of the Written Language

"Precisely what kind of unpleasantness happens to you and other Jews?" the foreigner asks.

"Unpleasantness at work: They dismissed me from my job as head of a department. Unpleasantness in science: VAK rejected the dissertation of my student.[3] It has become difficult to publish papers, to participate in conferences. One does not even dream about scientific trips abroad. Jews are not admitted to many universities, nor to graduate study. It is hard to find suitable work."

"So why don't you protest? If people act unjustly, appeal to their superiors. If there are laws against racial discrimination, then go to court. If you do not agree with the newspaper article of Etlis, then you should write an article for the newspaper. There will be an investigation, the facts will become public, and truth and justice will triumph."

I become angry.

"You are like a blind man in a strange room," I reply. "People do not get admitted to the university because they fail the entrance examinations. They don't get work because there are no jobs. Their dissertations are rejected because the quality is poor. You would be ridiculed if you claimed that the nationality of the candidate had any significance. Not one court would undertake an investigation of a case involving the persecution of nationalities because no such thing occurs here. Nor would you succeed with the newspapers."

"And freedom of speech?"

"It is guaranteed by the constitution, but you still cannot say that something exists that should not exist. No one would permit you to do so. My misfortunes increase a hundred times because they are like a disgraceful disease that I cannot discuss in public. To do so would put my life in danger. Work, science, family—everything would be in disarray. My freedom and life would be threatened. To begin to speak, to leave the crowd of silent people, to rise

---

3. VAK is the Higher Certification Commission, a government body that must approve all Candidate and Doctor of Sciences degrees conferred in the Soviet Union.—Ed.

up against society—for goodness sake, I want to live in peace, to work in peace. I have accumulated many theorems that I need to prove. Excuse me. I am a coward. I am simply afraid."

I have spent many long hours with such thoughts. How should I act? What should I do? Finally, I decided to write down my personal experiences. The written word has more than once been of enormous use to historians and has helped to change attitudes and customs. Perhaps this time too. . . .

# II. Studies (in the past . . .)

## A Documentary Poem

After graduating from the university, I started work in a scientific research institute, though I really wanted to study mathematics. The job was exhausting. I worked long hours, and in the evening I could not study. I began to go to sleep at eight in the evening and to wake up at three or four in the morning. That gave me four hours to study mathematics with a clear head. I did this every day for a year and a half. This period, from the exposure of the cosmopolitans to the notorious doctor-assassins, was for me, a Jew, extremely difficult.[1] Here are the documents. Judge for yourself.

*August 1, 1951.* From G. P. Svishev, deputy head of the Institute, to Academician I. G. Petrovskii, rector of Moscow State University: "The N. E. Zhukovskii Institute has no objection to the admission of G. A. Freiman, an employee of the Institute, as an external graduate student at Moscow State University."

From Deputy Director Lidskii to Comrade Freiman: "The Admissions Committee has decided not to give you permission to take the entrance examinations because you have not completed the work requirement. Three years of employment are required."

*April 16, 1952.* From G. A. Freiman, employee of the Central State Aviation Institute, to Academician I. G. Petrovskii, rector of Moscow State University: "I request permission to take the gradu-

1. Near the end of his life, Stalin began a purge of "rootless cosmopolitans," mostly Jews. In January, 1953, nine doctors were arrested, seven of them Jewish, and charged with murdering Zhdanov and other Soviet officials. Stalin died in March, 1953.—Ed.

ate qualifying examinations in mathematics in the Faculty of Mechanics and Mathematics."

Resolutions: "The examinations in mathematics can be arranged in the Institute of Mechanics and Mathematics. Please provide the authorization to take the examinations," (signed) A. Kolmogorov. "I recommend admission as an external graduate student," (signed) I. Petrovskii, May 15, 1952.

*June 12, 1952*. From G. A. Freiman, employee of the Central State Aviation Institute, to Academician I. G. Petrovskii, rector of Moscow State University: "Please enroll me as a graduate student in the Department of Number Theory of the Faculty of Mechanics and Mathematics."

*August 8, 1952*. From P. Yakovlev, deputy director and assistant professor, to Comrade G. A. Freiman: "We are returning your documents because the Kazan Aviation Institute has not approved your request for graduate study."

Extract from the minutes of the fourth meeting of the Admissions Committee of the Institute of Mechanics and Mathematics of Moscow State University on August 16, 1952: "Applicant: Freiman, Grigori Abelevich. Born 1926. Jew. Member of the Communist Party. Graduated Moscow State University in 1949. Mathematician. Employed at the Central State Aviation Institute for three years. Diploma without honors. (External graduate student.) Resolution: We recommend that he enroll as a graduate student at the Central State Aviation Institute.

"This extract is accurate," (signed) Uspenskaya, Secretary of the Institute.

*August 20, 1952*. From G. A. Freiman to Academician I. G. Petrovskii, rector of Moscow State University: "In 1949 I graduated from *Mekhmat*[2] of Moscow State University and was assigned to work at the Central State Aviation Institute (TsAGI). My educa-

---

2. *Mekhmat* is the Faculty of Mechanics and Mathematics —Ed.

tion is in mathematics. After working three years in TsAGI, I applied this year for graduate study in mathematics at Moscow State University. The Admissions Committee recommended that I 'enroll as a graduate student at TsAGI.' But at TsAGI there is only a graduate program in mechanics. Because I have received specialized training in mathematics, because I have continued to do research in mathematics for the last three years, and because I wish to continue to do research in mathematics in the future, I request that you reconsider my application and allow me to take the entrance examinations for graduate study."

*August 20, 1952.* From I. G. Petrovskii: "I see no reason to alter the decision of the Commission."

*August 20, 1952.* From G. A. Freiman to the director of the Kazan Pedagogical Institute: "I request permission to take the examinations for graduate study in mathematics."

*August 25, 1952.* From (signature illegible) to G. A. Freiman: "Your request is refused because you lack work experience in a school."

*August 30, 1952.* From Kharlamova, head of graduate studies at Kazan State University, to Comrade G. A. Freiman: "You will be permitted to take the entrance examinations for graduate study at Kazan State University. These examinations begin September 1, 1952."

*October 29, 1952.* From S. Semin, deputy head of the Central Administration of Universities, to Professor D. Ya. Martynov, rector of Kazan State University: "The Central Administration of Universities cannot allow the enrollment of Comrade G. A. Freiman as a graduate student because he has not been approved by the Graduate Admissions Committee."

*November 19, 1952.* From G. A. Freiman to Comrade Semin, deputy head of the Central Administration of Universities: "In your letter to Comrade Martynov, rector of Kazan State University, you wrote that I could not be enrolled as a graduate student because I have 'not been approved by the Graduate Admissions Committee.' Since I received the grade of 'excellent' on all of the entrance examinations and since I was allowed to register as a graduate student by the Committee of Kazan State University, I request that you inform me of the reason for my rejection by the Ministerial Committee."

Author's remark: I received no reply to this letter.

*December 25, 1952.* From G. A. Freiman to M. A. Prokof'ev, deputy minister of Higher Education: "In September, 1952, I took the entrance examinations for graduate study at Kazan University and was accepted by the University's Admissions Committee. However, my candidacy was not approved in the Ministry. For two months I have been trying unsuccessfully to learn the reason for my rejection. According to Comrade Semin and to Comrade Khitrov, who is dealing with my case directly, there are no documents stating the reason why I was rejected. Clearly, in these circumstances, the rejection is illegal.

"I believe that my rejection is unjustified for the following reasons: (1) I received the grade 'excellent' on all of the entrance examinations; (2) I have published seven scientific papers; (3) I have satisfied the requirement of three years work in industry before admission to graduate study; (4) My place of employment has given me positive recommendations regarding my work and Party duties; (5) Finally, it is important to note that I am a member of the Communist Party of the Soviet Union and a veteran of the Patriotic War [World War II].

"Consideration of my case has already lasted three months. I urge you to intervene personally to find out the reason for my rejection by the Ministry, to stop the bureaucratic meddling in my case, and, finally, to approve my enrollment in graduate school."

*Received January 20, 1953.* From Professor M. V. Markov, prorector for scientific work, Kazan State University, to G. A. Freiman: "Enclosed is a copy of the order to enroll you as a graduate student in this University."

*Studies (in the past . . .)*

Nowadays I am amazed at how persistent I was then, with a persistence rooted in the firm conviction in the propriety of everything that took place. It seemed to me that any impropriety must be purely accidental.

How much work, energy, and time I wasted on this business. To obtain any official letter, I had to waste days or weeks, arranging for interviews and standing in line.

And references! My boss, Yura Vasil'ev, was a harsh person who exploited his colleagues mercilessly. He had no wish to let me go. So as a result of some collective sophistry, the following remarks were included in my letter of recommendation: "It should be noted, however, that Comrade G. A. Freiman does not always show a conscientious attitude to his work. He has a formal attitude to this work, which, for some reason, he dislikes, notwithstanding its importance. He does not always show the necessary initiative. . . . He expresses a persistent desire to pursue graduate study in pure mathematics. This has been detrimental to his basic work."

And the conversation with Petrovskii!

Ivan Georgievich Petrovskii, the rector of Moscow State University, was himself a mathematician. In the summer of 1943 he was the dean of Mekhmat. I first met him when I transferred from Kazan University to Moscow University. He made a most pleasant impression on me. He talked quite slowly, showed an interest in the person to whom he was speaking and in his plans and concerns. He was at that time a thin man, intelligent, subtle, and compassionate. And now Petrovskii had agreed to see me because my teacher, Aleksandr Osipovich Gel'fond, had recommended me as a promising young student.

He received me in his large office in an old building of Moscow University on the Mokhovaya. I told him of my plight and of my great desire to pursue mathematics. Petrovskii listened carefully and, I thought, with some concern.

"It is too late now to change the decision of the Admissions Committee," he said.

"What about becoming an external student if I can't enroll as a regular student," I interrupted.

"No, you won't be able to do that either. Here's what I think," he said after a little thought. "You ought to pass your graduate qualifying examinations."

I realized that this seemingly omnipotent man was not prepared to see anything my way. Petrovskii, the friend and fellow student of my teacher and, most important, a mathematician, should have understood my strong desire to study the science we both loved.

"I don't understand what's going on," I shouted with some bitterness. "If I go to the left, you send me to the right. If I go to the right, you send me to the left. Where am I supposed to go?"

He did not understand what I was talking about and gave me a questioning look.

"You advise me take the graduate qualifying examinations and not apply for graduate school. But look what you wrote when I asked you for permission to take those examinations."

And I handed him my request to take the graduate qualifying examinations, along with his response: "I recommend admission as an external graduate student. I. Petrovskii, May 15, 1952."

He read it and said nothing. He sat motionless and did not say a word. I too remained silent, at first in agitation, then, when I had calmed down, in tense expectation of an answer. But he continued to sit motionless and in silence. This went on for at least three minutes. To me it seemed an eternity. Finally, in response to some uncontrollable impulse, and not wishing to interrupt this silent confession with hypocritical small talk, and also perhaps from a feeling of pity, I got up, took the paper from him, folded it, put it in my pocket, and walked out without even saying a word. He did not even stir.

I saw him one other time, exactly ten years later, when I went to see him with some request about the allocation of rooms in the student dormitory at Moscow University. He was a completely different person. He had aged and put on a lot of weight. But more than that, he seemed harassed, nervous, and preoccupied. He did not listen to what I was saying. He did not even grasp what I was saying. With scarcely an idea about what the request was about, he turned it down on the spot, rudely and brusquely and allowing no appeal, as if he were feverishly preoccupied with his own problems.

## Studies (in the past . . .)

And finally the graduate school at Kazan!

When I received the letter of rejection from the Ministry, I was stunned, but nonetheless I was firmly convinced that I could prove the justice of my case. They could not turn me down. It was as simple as that.

I went to the Ministry to see Khitrov in the personnel department. He was an elderly man with gray hair and a military bearing. He showed no particular ill feeling of unpleasantness towards me.

"This Committee has rejected your application," he said.

That was the most that I was ever able to squeeze out of him on that as well as on succeeding occasions. They had the decision, but nothing more. No explanation, no minutes of the meeting, not even my documents. Everything had been sent back. I should go back to Kazan. The matter had been decided.

"The decision will be reconsidered," I said firmly. "There are not the slightest grounds for a rejection."

He remained adamant, but gradually something began to happen. They asked for my personal files from Kazan. Khitrov sent reports about me to several departments. Although the situation had not changed, I began to overpower Khitrov psychologically. When he saw me, he would become nervous and would suggest in an uneasy voice that I leave, that the matter was hopeless.

"The Committee has turned you down," he would say emphatically. "There is nothing you can do."

I would just remain perfectly calm, reassuring him that my case was just and that the decision would be changed.

Finally I managed to get an interview with the assistant to the deputy minister. He heard my case in a room in which several women were sitting. I laid all my trump cards directly on the table: Grades of "excellent" in the examinations, all my published works, etc. etc. A hush fell over the room as the women, feigning indifference, listened to my story.

"I will arrange a meeting for you with Prokof'ev," the assistant said.

Prokof'ev listened carefully and then said that there would be a meeting of the committee the next day. He said that my case should be considered for approval.

I waited a day and then went to see Khitrov.

"Yes, they have reconsidered your case and approved your application," he said in an embarrassed voice. "I will prepare the notification. When would you prefer it to be dated?"

That was the beginning of January, 1953, and we agreed to date it from the eleventh. Two days later, on January 13, the affair of the "doctor-assassins" broke out and a shadow fell over everything. It affected me personally very little. I was admitted to graduate school. I went to Kazan and began the serious study of mathematics.

For those who do not understand or who pretend not to understand the reality of the events I have described, I shall add a pair of vivid impressions of that time.

## The Yellow Star

Misha Klyachko was a small, uncomely, sluggish person with a quiet voice. I remember him in contrast to his wife, who was large and attractive with red lips.

We were discussing the admission of Misha to the Communist party. He had been through the war and had become a candidate member of the Party while at the front. There was nothing in his past to raise any doubts, but there was one discrepancy in his documents. In his Party document, the candidate membership card, he was registered as Russian, but in his passport he was registered as Jewish. At the Party meeting called to decide his membership, he was asked to explain this discrepancy. Misha explained that when he got out of the hospital after being wounded he was given new Red Army identification papers in which he wrote that he was Russian.

"And why did you register as Russian?" asked Ogibalov, the Party representative in *Mekhmat*, who then and subsequently has played a most sinister role in faculty affairs. I remember his face, always sullen and hostile with vacant evasive eyes and a dry accusatory voice.

Misha became confused and muttered incoherently, but despite the strong pressure he was unable to explain anything. He fell silent while in his mind's eye a fantastic scene swam by. A German in an SS uniform comes running into the auditorium, grabs hold of him, and starts to drag him to the door. But the door is no longer a door. It is an open gas chamber behind which he could see the roaring ovens of Auschwitz. Ogibalov jumps up from behind his table and starts pushing him towards the chamber.

A short debate ensued. A young fellow with a thick head of curly hair, wearing a pair of crumpled trousers and with a perfectly good-natured face, jumped up onto the stage. He made an impassioned and convincing speech that there was no reason for any controversy, that in our country there are no distinctions between peoples of different nationalities, and that it is just as honorable to be a Jew as a Russian. Therefore, Misha should be accepted into the Party. Both the auditorium and the Presidium listened to all this in a polite, somewhat strained silence. Then a member of the Party Bureau got up and said that of course they were only concerned with a formal discrepancy in the documents that required immediate correction. Klyachko's application, however, would have to be rejected. And that was the decision.

Not long ago I saw the new version of the internal Soviet passport. It no longer contains the entry for "social origin," which used to confer different privileges to the representatives of different social classes. But the entry for "nationality," which did not exist in the years immediately following the Russian Revolution, has been retained in the new passport. The story of Klyachko illustrates how the nationality entry can be used for evil purposes. Can anyone explain to me how such an entry could possibly be used in the service of the noble ideals of universal brotherhood?

## The Alliance of the Sword and the Ploughshare

When I was a student in the fifth year at the university, an "anti-Soviet organization" was discovered in our midst.

What really happened? There was a small group of boys and girls who had been close friends since their first year in the university. They often got together and strolled through the streets discussing works of art and, in particular, criticizing Surov's play "The Green Street." (This became an important point in the prosecution.) As a joke they invented a set of rules for their group. (This is an organization for you!)

Nadya Gindina had an uncle who lived in Palestine. This uncle mailed her a large book, a scientific treatise on either botany or zoology, that her father needed for his work. I remember well the enormous attention that Gorbunov devoted to this book. Gorbunov, the secretary of the Party Bureau, made a speech at a general meeting of all the fifth-year students. What an evil character this event acquired in his interpretation! What noxious fumes of alien incursions, apostasy, and espionage began to waft over the tense silence in the hall.

The whole thing was set off by some poem about Jews that no one ever saw.

There were twelve people in the group, six Jews and six Russians. Just like the campaign against the "cosmopolitans," it was conducted not against Jews only, but on the whole it was the Jews who were punished. The others were let off lightly.

All the Jews were expelled from the Komsomol and from the university. The others just received a reprimand from the Komsomol.

Those who actively organized the persecution—Ogibalov, Gorbunov, and Gusarova—are still working at the university and prospering.

# III. Studies (. . . and in the present)

## Difficulties in Higher Education

Am I just stirring up the distant past? No. My story is timely. If I were to enter graduate school today, my experience would be just the same.

What is it like to apply for admission to an institution of higher education today? At the time of my own unfortunate experiences, practically no Jews at all were admitted to *Mekhmat* at Moscow State University. Then came the "Thaw." But in 1970 there was a new sharp turn for the worse and the admission of Jews to *Mekhmat* stopped almost completely. At one meeting devoted to the beginning of a new academic year, Ogibalov said, "Finally we have the kind of entering class that we have been trying to get for a long time."

What is it like in other institutions of higher education?

In the Moscow Engineering and Physics Institute and in the Moscow Physical and Technical Institute, there have always been strict quotas. There are also quotas in many other institutions: military, diplomatic (of course), medical (except those in outlying areas), and military technical (aviation and electronics). There are even stricter quotas in certain places, such as the Ukraine, Moldavia, and Leningrad. This list, of course, is not complete.

One can certainly argue that Jews in Russia have by no means been forced into the depths of ignorance, that there are far more Jews than Russians in higher education relative to their numbers in the population, and that even now the number of Jewish students is very great.

This situation developed earlier, however, when the quotas were not so severe. Now things are changing rapidly "for the better."

At the present time the quotas exist and are getting worse.

What is the mechanism for this? Is there no control over the classification of documents according to their nationality?

Only with rare exceptions. If a job is in any way connected with secret material, an undesirable individual is sometimes advised not to apply. Even a high score on the entrance examinations does not guarantee admission. For example, *F* passed the entrance examinations for the Moscow Physical and Technical Institute with the highest grade in his group and . . . he did not find his name on the list of those accepted. Outside the office of the Admissions Committee there was an announcement: "No inquiries will be accepted concerning admissions."

This, however, is not the most dishonest thing. It is worse when a person is deliberately given failing grades in the examinations despite the high level of his answers.

A foreigner visiting the Soviet Union and hearing about these things for the first time might say, "This is strange. After all, a professor, a teacher, is a responsible individual with a considerable degree of professional dignity and well-developed standards for work. Are you telling me that such a person consciously cheats, juggles his grades? Good heavens. That is like a doctor who consciously kills his patients."

"As far as doctors are concerned, I don't know. But there are teachers who have deserted the ethics of their profession and who let themselves be guided by other, more selfish principles."

"You need to have some substantial proof for that opinion, as well as for the existence of quotas."

"As far as the situation in one particular field is concerned, I know all the details. At Moscow University in 1949, the year I graduated, at least one-fourth of the students in my class were Jewish. Later on, in the fifties and sixties, the proportion scarcely ever fell below one-fifth. The other day I looked through the list of second-year students in *Mekhmat* and did not find a single Jewish name. Two years ago the list of students admitted to the *Mekhmat* of Leningrad University contained several hundred people, but I found no more than two or three Jewish names. The trend is clear and indisputable. If these assertions should ever be debated, let my critics disclose to the public the composition by nationality of the students in *Mekhmat* year by year since the end of the war. The evidence is incontrovertible.

"These facts have a broader significance because Moscow and Leningrad Universities, as well as the Novosibirsk University, which also discriminates against Jews, turn out the lion's share of the creative research mathematicians."

"Wouldn't it be better to examine these facts in detail? But how did you go about it? Was it any of your business? You calculated a few percentages, read a few lists, examined the family names. You would be better off proving your theorems."

"But the human being? The living soul?" I shouted in exasperation. "Look at the journal *Kvant*. In issue after issue you will find the names of the school children who have won prizes for solving problems. This is still done objectively, since Shirshov and his cohorts have not yet managed to dominate the journal completely. Follow the fate of these children. How many of them, the children who could be the pride of our science, will end up doing some hum-drum job in the office of some small, rural factory? And will not our country be the loser if, in desperation, one of these youngsters decides to emigrate?

"And what about science? What will happen to mathematics? The nurturing of talent and the creation of scientific schools is a delicate affair requiring many years of work and effort. It grows like a forest grows."

He who chops down the forest will see a desert.

## The Mechanism of Rejection

You could ask: Why do I believe that the examinations are conducted unfairly, since I have never been present in person?

My first impressions were the result of an accumulation of verbal testimony. Here are some examples.

The son of the famous mathematician *K* was taking the entrance examinations for *Mekhmat*.

"My son is very good at mathematics, and I am not worried about that. But his physics is not that good, and he might only get a four."[1]

The son received a two in physics.

Here you could object that parents always overestimate their children's abilities and that, perhaps, the examiners were not unfair.

V passed both his exams in mathematics with grade five, and physics, which was a tricky exam, with grade four. He received a two, however, for an essay that was written without any mistakes. The reason: "You have brought out the theme of patriotism, but you failed to develop the theme of the Motherland."

This case was later described as follows: "Jews are not admitted to *Mekhmat*, that's the way it is, but in this case, you know, that was going too far. That's why V passed." A teacher at Moscow University, and a Russian, told this to some people who were not even his close acquaintances.

Z received the first prize in the All-Union Mathematical Olympiad, but only a two in the entrance examination in mathematics.

Why is such a discrepancy unbelievable?

The winner of such an Olympiad is the best mathematician among millions. The problems are so difficult that by no means all the professors can solve them and certainly not in such a short time.

I could multiply the number of such examples. I know hundreds. But let us restrict ourselves to these for now. What kind of people are they who deliberately give out these undeserved grades of "two?" How do they do it?

There are always scoundrels. Honest people just look upon them with disapproval and say nothing. But I first heard how it was actually done in a conversation with R, who worked at Novosibirsk University. At a faculty party one of his colleagues who served on the Admissions Committee began a heart-to-heart conversation with him. He dissociated himself from all of this. He did not do it.

---

1. In the Soviet Union, examinations are graded from five (the highest score) down to two (the lowest score). Two is the failing grade.—Ed.

This was done by special people who examined the groups in which Jewish applicants were concentrated.

The moral aspect of these facts is extraordinarily acute. Can one draw conclusions based only on hearsay, no matter how indisputable it might appear?

In August of this year I frequently visited *Mekhmat* and could follow the course of the entrance examinations. I can thus share the results of my personal observations.

I was acquainted with many people who were working in Moscow University to prepare to take the exams. There is much preexamination discussion. A day before the oral exam, I again heard the rumor that Jews were being concentrated in special groups. What is the method used to sift them out? Superficially the exam goes entirely normally. Everything is very simple. The students are asked to solve problems, but more difficult problems than the usual ones.

We must consider now in more detail what is a difficult problem and what is an easy one, and also how we can measure the degree of difficulty.

In another field, for example, in chemistry, I could easily play the role of a distraught parent whose child complains that a problem is too difficult. The distraught father goes to the secretary of the Admissions Committee.

"A difficult problem?" says the secretary. "But that's the purpose of a university. We have to solve difficult problems."

"But that problem was *too* difficult," the parent insists, feeling himself lost in a fog. "They never solved anything like that at school."

"No, it was not too difficult," the specialist explains with condescending patience towards the father's incompetence. "We cannot set standard problems. We do not take everybody, only the best."

And papa goes away, not exactly satisfied, but knowing that there is nothing he can say. To measure human potential, one needs knowledge and experience.

Sometimes it is not nearly so difficult to work out objective criteria. For example, let us take ability in the high jump as a way of measuring physical fitness. Neither you, the reader, nor I am a specialist, but we can nonetheless make the most elementary judgments.

If you cannot jump over:

125 cm.—You gave up sports long ago and now enjoy nothing better than a good dinner.

150 cm.—It should be easy for anyone to jump this high.

If you can jump over:

175 cm.—This is noteworthy and shows good potential.

200 cm.—Incredible! You are the hope of Soviet sports. Almost no one in the whole country can clear this height.

225 cm.—Impossible, this does not happen. This is too good to be true.

Although this all appears simple, the specialist sees far more. He measures the test in terms of centimeters. He evaluates technique, previous training, and future potential. When he sees a well-proportioned young athlete fly over the high bar with ease, the old trainer's heart beats faster in joyous anticipation. This pupil, blessed with a remarkable talent, for whom he has waited so long, will absorb the wisdom and experience gained over many years and go on to conquer new heights.

Suddenly, instead of the touching figure of the old devoted teacher, another very different character crawls out, sullen and watchful.

"What is your last name?" he asks. "Airanetyan? Tsoi? Rozentsveig? Ugh, more Armenian brats, yellow faces, Yiddish snouts. Well, then, in the written exam you jumped 175 centimeters? Now here's another question. Let's see you jump ten centimeters higher. You made it? Raise the bar another two meters! Can't you do it now? Give him a two! Next!"

When the criteria are not so easily discernible, the sense of the preceding remarks still applies.

What constitutes a difficult problem in mathematics? Can it be measured? It is not easy, but it is possible. It is done by a system of expert grading. For example, I have examined thousands of school children, participated in and presided over numerous Olympiads. I have set the problems for entrance examinations. If I work out a scale of difficulty with which all conscientious specialists agree, then the nonspecialist can trust it. Here I would like to give examples of problems of five levels of difficulty.[2]

*Problem 1.* Construct the graph of the function[3]
$$y = |x|.$$

*Problem 2.* Prove that the number
$$\log_2 3$$
is irrational.

*Problem 3.* Solve the equation
$$\sqrt{a + \sqrt{a + x}} = x, \text{ where } a > 0.$$

*Problem 4.* In a given triangle, a circle is inscribed, around which is circumscribed a square. Prove that the triangle contains more than half the perimeter of the square.

*Problem 5.* The numbers $m$ and $n$ have the same prime divisors. The numbers $m - 1$ and $n - 1$ also have the same prime divisors. Is there a finite or an infinite number of such pairs of integers $m$ and $n$?

The student gets these problems and starts to solve them.

*Problem 1.* "Here on the right we have the symbol for absolute value," says the schoolchild with average ability. "Let us use the definition. Thus,
$$y = \begin{cases} x \text{ if } x \geq 0 \\ -x \text{ if } x < 0. \end{cases}$$
Hence, we have the picture

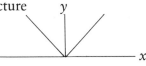

2. Those who find this section difficult can skip the mathematical material. But some people want to get to the heart of the matter and take nothing on trust.

3. To eliminate those who can reproduce the solution to this problem from memory without understanding the meaning, one can pose this problem in a slightly altered form, for example:
$$y = |2x - 1|.$$

"We did this problem in school," he will say if you ask him. "I knew how to solve it."

Let us digress from the theme of these remarks and consider the following question.

"How many of our secondary school graduates can solve this problem?" I ask.

"All three million of them can solve it," answers the inspector of the Ministry of Education. After thinking a little more, he adds, "Of course, there are pupils who have not satisfied the requirements of the syllabus, but they are very few."

For many years I have struggled against the low level of training in mathematics, and I know well how bad the situation is. I believe that two out of three[4] of our secondary school graduates could not solve a problem of this type.[5]

*Problem 2.* "Let us try to give a proof by contradiction," say the best-prepared students. All of the cleverness required to do this problem is contained in this sentence. From here on it is easy. If

$$\log_2 3 = \frac{p}{q}, \text{ where } p > 0, q > 0,$$

then

$$2^{p/q} = 3, \text{ and so } 2^p = 3^q.$$

But $2^p$ is an even number and $3^q$ is an odd number, hence they cannot be equal, and we have obtained a contradiction.

The average level of those who entered Moscow University this year, 1976, was not very high, and the level of difficulty of the questions asked in the oral examinations was not very high. Except in special cases.

*Problem 3.* "Let us remove the radicals," says the schoolboy as he begins to work on the problem.

$$a + \sqrt{a + x} = x^2$$
$$\sqrt{a + x} = x^2 - a$$
$$a + x = x^4 - 2ax^2 + a^2$$
$$x^4 - 2ax^2 - x + a^2 - a = 0.$$

4. Even specialists would not expect this result. The tests given by the Ministry of Education yield a completely different and more optimistic result, but they, as a rule, are falsified.

5. See footnote 3.

"We have obtained a fourth-degree equation," he says, "and I don't know how to solve such equations."

"Try introducing a new variable," suggests the conscientious teacher. "Denote $\sqrt{a + x}$ by $y$."

To think of a trick like this is not easy, but with the trick it is simple. Since $\sqrt{a + x} = y$ and $\sqrt{a + y} = x$, where $x \geqslant 0$ and $y \geqslant 0$, it follows that $y - x = x^2 - y^2$.

Since the relation $x + y = -1$ is impossible, it follows that $y - x = 0$, hence $y = x$ and so $x^2 - x - a = 0$. Therefore,

$$x = \frac{1 + \sqrt{4a + 1}}{2}.$$

How many students are capable of solving this problem? A thousand, perhaps. Two thousand? Hardly.

This problem might be given in the entrance examinations to *Mekhmat* at Moscow State University if there were a very stiff competition. But it was used only in special cases.

*Problem 4.* This problem is not at all standard. You will probably find only a few dozen children in the entire country who can solve it. I did it in three different ways over a period of several days, but at first it was not at all clear to me how to go about it. A colleague of mine, an assistant professor of geometry, worked on it for three days. When he solved it, he telephoned me specially from Kalinin.

The basic difficulty is guessing that the solution is obtained from the following problem: A circle of radius $R$ is inscribed in a square. What is the length of the largest part of the perimeter of the square that can be cut off by a tangent to the circle?

It is possible to solve this extremal problem and prove that the maximal length is cut off by a tangent perpendicular to the diagonal of the square. This maximum is $2(2 - \sqrt{2})R$. Thus, in the original problem, the triangle cuts off no more than $6(2 - \sqrt{2})R \approx 3.5R$ from the perimeter of the square. But the perimeter of the square is $8R$, and more than $4.4R$ of this remains, i.e. more than half.

Only the most ill-intentioned people would give this problem on an entrance examination and this year it was given. In special cases.

*Problem 5.* This is a problem of incredible difficulty at the high school level. It would be impossible even to ask this question in the Mathematical Olympiads. I could not solve it after working at it for an hour, though I think I would be able to do it after a few days of systematic work. Someone gave me the answer, but it is not clear how the answer was obtained:
$$m = 2^k - 1, n = (2^k - 1)^2.$$
Sasha Novodvorskii was given this problem in last year's entrance examinations for *Mekhmat*. His stepbrother recently emigrated to Israel. On the written examination Sasha got a five, but on the oral examination only a two.

What was the average difficulty of the problems this year?

Gavrilova was given problem 2 and also this problem: Prove that $3 < \pi < 4$.

Gavrilov got the following problems. Construct the graph of the function
$$y = 2^{\log_2 x}.$$
Construct a line segment equidistant between two intersecting lines. Find the range of the function
$$y = \frac{x}{x^2 + 1}$$
These problems are all of the second level of difficulty.

Are these examples typical? Yes. While the oral examinations in mathematics were being conducted, other applicants and their anxious and curious parents crowded around the *Mekhmat* offices. They immediately accosted those coming out and showered them with questions. The puzzled mamas asked them to repeat every word and wrote down all of the problems that were asked in the exams. I can summarize my own observations of more than twenty people.

1. In more than half the cases, the grade in the oral exam was higher than in the written. It was never lower.

2. In the majority of cases, the level of difficulty of the problems was that of level two and occasionally of a level between two and three. Never more difficult.

Now for the special cases.

Rubinshtein was asked problem 4 from our list of problems on his oral examination. He had worked on it for fifteen minutes when the examiner came up and asked if he had finished! Then he was given another problem, a complicated variant of problem 3. Finkel'shtein also was asked both of these questions.

Also significant are the results of the examinations inflicted upon several students from Mathematical School Number 2, a school whose exceptionally talented graduates usually continue on to *Mekhmat*.[6]

I had already heard brilliant reports about Yura Sorkin. He won the first prize in the All-Union Mathematical Olympiad, but did not go on to the International Olympiad because of some strange administrative difficulty. What do you think would happen if Ol'ga Korbut were not allowed to enter an athletics institute because she had failed an examination in athletics. There could be only one result. Ol'ga would be accepted and the unfortunate examiner would be fired. But Yura did not pass the examinations. In the oral exam he was given three problems of the fourth level of difficulty, among them the following: Which is greater: $\sin(8/7)$ or $8\pi/27$? Yura solved this problem. This alone should be enough to get a five, the highest grade. Another problem they slipped him had been presented by Yugoslavia in an International Mathematical Olympiad.

Beskin, Verkhovskii, Illarionov (Shapiro), Lipkin, and Fleishman also failed the examinations. All of their problems were of the fourth level of difficulty. Each of them, except Fleishman, had to solve the same problem, described above, that had been given to Sorkin. The numbers considered in that problem are equal, respectively, to 0.910 and 0.931. How could a student in secondary school distinguish between them without the use of tables? I find it difficult to imagine. This is only in the power of a *wunderkind* like Sorkin.

Thus there exists a special examination: "Difficult problems for Jews." In these special cases, as a rule, the results in the oral examination were lower than in the written, never higher. In the usual cases, it was the reverse.

6. Mathematical School Number 2 is a boarding school in Moscow for the most brilliant secondary school students in mathematics in the USSR. It has had a reputation of being a breeding ground for dissidents.—Ed.

## A "Misunderstanding"

Yura Sorkin is a Russian. His father is only half Jewish and is registered as Russian in his passport. His mother is pure Russian. The boy was considered Jewish, however, and the appropriate special procedure was used when he applied to *Mekhmat*. Many professors on the faculty knew his father, the mathematician Yurii Isaakovich Sorkin, and the logical conclusions were drawn. The people doing this, you see, are concerned citizens who are motivated by the "dictates of the heart" and who try to show initiative. They will not be fooled by an entry in a passport. They stare hard at the photograph, listen to the sound of the patronymic, and make inquiries.

When Yura's mother learned about the result of the examination, she went to the chairman of the Admissions Committee. He did not want to see her, but Sorkina is an energetic woman. She had once been an actress in a circus. She burst into his office and exclaimed, "It is a misunderstanding. There has been a misunderstanding. My son is not Jewish at all!"

And she explained the whole family tree. The professor went crimson and chased her out of his office, explaining all the time the just principles of our way of life.

Academician Kolmogorov interceded personally to get Sorkin admitted to the university, but even this did not help.

## The Mechanism of Rejection, Continued

In order to check how the candidates are arranged into examination groups, I went up to the fourteenth floor of the Moscow University building, where the Admissions Committee displays its notices. However, I was disappointed. There was no list of names. Applicants were designated by the numbers on their examination cards. What was to be done? I decided to carry out the check at another place, which was rumored to practice an analogous method of discrimination. I do not wish to name the particular institution of higher education nor the faculty involved, so I shall only discuss the results of my investigation.

# Studies (. . . and in the present)

At the entrance to the office of the Admissions Committee are three large bulletin boards with lists of the applicants who have taken the written examination in mathematics, about 1,160 persons.

The only information I had was the sound of the applicants' first and last names. I made some extracts from the lists. On the left is the name of the applicant. On the right is the number of his examination group.

1. Erivanskii, Yurii Konstantinovich 28
2. Liberman, Valentin Isaakevich 53
3. Kushnir, Valerii Vladimirovich 53
4. Shtern, Ol'ga Davidovna 28
. . . . . . . . . . . . . . . . . . . . . . . . . . . . . . . . . .
35. Konikov, Arkadii Bentsionovich 16
36. Grinbaum, Semen Matveevich 41

The thirty-six people on my list were distributed into groups in the following way:

| | |
|---|---|
| 1 person in a group | 8 groups |
| 2 persons in a group | 6 groups |
| 3 persons in a group | 1 group |
| 6 persons in a group | 1 group |
| 7 persons in a group | 1 group |

If thirty-six persons are distributed randomly among sixty groups, then, as a rule, any single group should not contain more than one person from our list. A cluster of two or more would be improbable. But that is exactly what I came across immediately with the two groups 53 and 28, and with even larger clusters. Liberman—53, Kushnir—53. These names were next to each other on the list and so I remembered the number 53. Soon I came across it again. Pinchuk, . . . Izrailevna—53, Zakharevich, . . . Itskovich—53, Kogan, . . . Efimovich—53, . . . . These members of group 53 were close together on the list. The rest of the group consisted of last names that did not "grate the ear." I found a similar situation with group 28. Coincidence? At first glance it is hard to decide. Then I remembered that I am a mathematician and I calculated the probability. It was less than $10^{-19}$. Is it possible three times in a row to guess successfully five numbers out of thirty-six in a lottery?

So it turned out that there was nothing coincidental at all in the way in which my thirty-six people had been arranged in groups.

Only three people on my list passed the entrance examinations. The probability of this occurring is 1 out of 100,000. Only one Jewish applicant passed out of every twelve, whereas the average was one out of two.

What are the motives of those who perpetrate this? They are not new. What do we call it when socialism is not intended for everyone? There is one perpetrator in Moscow University. His name is Ul'yanov. Once when he was drunk at a postdissertation party, he said aloud, "You are not a bad fellow, and I have nothing against you. But we are at home here and we don't need you."[7]

There are two fine and intelligent boys, Slechka T. and Kostya N. Ya., in their first year at Kalinin University, who meet with me once a week. They are interested in everything—solving difficult problems, listening to different things in mathematics. I enjoy working with them. But is it really worthwhile to spend my time with them? You see, Petr Lavrent'evich Ul'yanov, a foreign member of the American Mathematical Society, is ready to make their lives miserable. Well, I shall carry on with my work. Maybe some day Russians will be found who will keep him under control.

---

7. This reminds me of the words of Count Mentirov, a minister of the Tsar, as reported by S. A. Stepnyak-Kravchinskii: "I am warmly disposed toward the Jews. Our western border is open to you. Do us a favor. Europe is at your service. That is where there is a place for you. That is where they love you. That is where they need your talents and abilities. What do we need them for? We have enough of our own. We need a Russian spirit."

# IV. Work

## Do you need work? So what?

After he was appointed head of a newly created Computer Center, G began to select personnel and asked the manager from the ministry to approve the candidates. G had chosen ten people to be department heads and two of them were Jews. The manager looked silently through the documents and put aside the files of the two Jewish applicants.

"They are not suitable."

"They are good specialists, Candidates of Science."

"So what?"

"We need those people very much."

"So what? We are choosing department heads. We would have to go with them to conferences, to the State Planning Committee, to the Council of Ministers. I would have to sit next to them. It's written all over their faces."

Here is another example of the same way of thinking. The philosopher Navskii, author of the book *History of Western Philosophy*, was trying to get elected to the Academy. He sent a letter to the president of the Academy that refuted the malicious rumor that he was a Jew, and he proved convincingly that he was a Pole. This wise man, however, still did not get into the Academy.

The following happened in Kalinin to the director of a school. He scolded one of the teachers, Nikol'skaya, at a staff meeting. Social status: her husband is a philologist and a professor. She could not take it and in front of the whole group she called the director a dirty Jew. He complained to the local committee of the Party. He tried to see the first secretary, but without success. They directed him to the local department of education. A commission came to the school and Nikol'skaya was given a reprimand for bad behavior, but the director . . . was removed from his job for slacking in the task of ideological education. It took him six months to find a job as a teacher somewhere in the suburbs.

Not long ago in a certain academic institute ten laboratories were closed, the heads of eight of which were Jews. This was certainly not coincidental. Not long before this the director had written an article for the newsletter of the institute. It stated: "the personnel policy of this administration will be changed in view of the large number of rejections by Soviet citizens." That may be, but why does no one get upset about the opposite situation? Surely here one has interchanged cause and effect.

This is a characteristic feature of recent times. In earlier years delicate subjects were discussed in Aesopian language. Nowadays, these subjects are more and more being discussed quite candidly.

A young specialist arrived at a research institute of the Soviet Academy of Sciences. With him was a personnel officer of the Institute, who initiated the following discussion in one of the corridors. Everyone overheard the conversation.

"So you're Russian?"

"Yes."

"And your mother and father? Are they both Russians?"

"Yes, both of them."

"And your wife? Russian?"

"Yes."

"Well, then, everything is fine."

I have recorded here only a few particularly amusing incidents. I have omitted many more ordinary incidents. It is not my goal to conduct an exhaustive investigation. I would like, however, to show just one more facet of my feeling of uselessness and personal isolation.

## Inspection day and my birthday

At the beginning of 1971, I boarded the electric train in Kalinin and wondered how long it would take me to get to my home in Troparev. It worked out to four hours. We passed the tall, typically

Moscow-style houses in Krykov and Klin, the deserted little forest that came right up to the station in Yamug, and the snow-covered expanse of the sea of Moscow that spread out on both sides of the railroad tracks and was interlaced with the chimneys of the Redkin chemical factory. From now on I would be able to contemplate this scene two days a week.

I reviewed my life up to now.

Some original work done in mathematics. Plus. But almost twenty years of working in the educational system had left me disillusioned. The generally low level of mathematical knowledge remains the same, and no effort on my part will change it. Minus. I have managed to move to Moscow. Plus. But I was not able to find a good job there. Minus.

The rector of Kalinin University could not make time to see me, but he approved my application without seeing me and I was hired. Later I found out indirectly that the director had serious doubts about offering me the job.

I have done a lot in the last four years. I have worked hard and with renewed enthusiasm. I discovered a new area of activity—applied mathematics.

At the time I started my new job, students were given only a twenty-hour course in computer programming, and they had to practice on an old M–3 vacuum tube computer.

Four years later:

In "my" area there are now about a hundred people. Kalinin University has a Computer Center with three large halls containing two M–220 and one ES–1020 computers. The Center has earned a quarter million rubles in consulting fees. The faculty of computational mathematics now has an extremely well qualified staff of teachers. My new speciality, applied mathematics, now has hundreds of students.

But soon they kicked me out.

The rector decides everything in the university. He holds everything tightly in his hands.

I believe that when I was hired to work there, it was not accidental that he avoided meeting me: "Right now you are working, but remember, it was not I who hired you."

The rector is generally well-regarded among his colleagues. He is intelligent, decisive, and not disposed to bow down to authorities. He respects scholars, or, more precisely, people with a Doctor of Sciences degree. He is tolerant of people of different nationalities. Moreover, he had given me a good job, did not interfere in my affairs, and I was grateful to him.

But in January, 1975, the rector unexpectedly ordered the splitting up of the Computer Center. Soon after, they took the scientific research section away from me. My two assistants were very instrumental in that. Both of them were retired colonels who did not get on very well with intellectuals, and they were very sensitive to questions of rank.

I involuntarily recalled an incident in my past. While I was living in Elabug, I went on an excursion conducted by the head of the Shishkin Museum, a woman who was a local resident with only a seventh-grade education.

"Shishkin was the greatest Russian landscape painter," she said.

"What about Levitan?" someone asked.

"Compared to Shishkin, Leviatan stinks," she said, offended. "Besides, he is a Jew."

And now for inspection day.

Several times our secretary had handed me requests from the Second Department[1] to go and see them. I finally went and saw that important work was going on.

"We must have your study plans and syllabi for inspection day."

I promised to drop them off later, then promptly forgot all about it.

One day I was told that if I did not deliver them, they would tell the rector. I swore to myself, tore myself away from my real work, collected my syllabi, and went to see them. We went to the end of a corridor and knocked on a small locked window. The door was unlocked, and we were led into a large room with iron bars on the windows. A man sat there with a totally expressionless face. A girl brought some papers from another room. There were two columns

1. This department is concerned with internal security and is connected with the KGB.—Ed.

on the papers. In the left column was a list of subjects and in the right were the class times. I told him that I knew what to do, when suddenly the man said casually, "By the way, we have decided to register you now." A paper appeared in his hand and he showed me where to sign.

I took the pen and was in the process of signing without paying much attention, when I suddenly noticed on this official government document phrases like "state secrets" and "foreign citizens." I took the form from the inspector's hands and began to read it carefully. I wondered what it was all about. It became clear that it concerned getting a security clearance for access to classified information. I expressed doubt about the necessity of my signing this document, since all of my work was unclassified.

"All of the department heads have signed the same form," the inspector said nonchalantly.

"It is written here that I must not divulge state secrets," I said. "I don't know any secrets and I don't want to know any. As for contact with foreigners, I maintain a large scientific correspondence. And what about trips abroad? I am interested in scientific contacts."

"We will examine the matter and give you special permission."

"It would be better not to get involved in this at all. Frankly, I have serious doubts. You know, this is a very serious document."

"It is indeed," he acknowledged, dropping his nonchalant tone for the first time.

"Well, I want to think about it carefully before I sign," I said, putting the paper back on the table.

"This will be reported to the rector."

"That is your business."

I excused myself and left.

We had both completely forgotten about checking the syllabi. But, of course, they were never really the issue.

I asked my colleagues and acquaintances. Nothing like this had happened to any of them. Had the whole performance been organized for just one spectator?

Soon, on a beautiful spring day, three women from my department came up to me and asked, "There is an announcement in the local newspaper that your job as head of the department of computational mathematics is available. What's going on?"

I told my colleague *J* about it.

"This is outrageous and unprecedented," he exclaimed. "I never heard anything like it. Didn't you satisfy all the requirements for the job?"

"Yes, over a year ago, and I was approved unanimously. They even buttered me up by calling me a 'magnificent administrator.'"

"Make a complaint and they will have to retract the announcement."

"Perhaps they would, but it is not worth protesting," I said. "The rector can find a hundred other reasons to throw me out. And I am more interested in the work I'm doing than in the title of my position."

Soon afterwards I approached the rector after a faculty meeting and asked to speak with him. He hesitated, saying how busy he was, but I insisted. He finally agreed and invited me into his office. The secretary of the Party Committee came in as well, but did not utter a word throughout the interview. He sat silently with a gloomy expression on his face.

I asked the rector to explain the announcement of the vacancy.

"I won't hide the fact that we are looking for a new man to head the department. But you know, you asked for this yourself. Only recently you were telling me that you would willingly give up applied mathematics and once again immerse yourself in your beloved number theory."

At this point I raised my voice for the first time and began to argue.

"I have never asked for anything of the kind. I agree I was about to start looking for a good young specialist and gradually hand over the job to him. But you have decided to fire me immediately. You should have discussed it with me first. I would have resigned the position and transferred to another department. Then you could have announced the vacancy. But now it looks like you fired me because I was incompetent. That's what everyone will think."

"Well, perhaps we did overlook something," the rector said. "If you wish, I will explain at a meeting of the Academic Council."

You will hardly do that, I thought.

"Well, you have obviously decided everything for me. I have no wish to cause trouble. Beginning in September I would like to transfer to the Faculty for Advanced Training."

And that's what happened.

What part did my nationality play in all of this? A very substantial role. The number of Jewish people in top positions is diminishing everywhere, including Kalinin State University. Five years ago there were about ten Jews who were department heads, but now only two or three. Would the rector have fired me if I was not a Jew? Possibly. He would never have done it so rudely, however, with no chance for me to appeal, and in violation of the law. He clearly felt that he was dealing with someone powerless, someone who will not raise a fuss, who has nowhere to go, to whom anything can be done. This is one of the reasons I am depressed now. I finally understood that they keep you around only as long as they need you. When they find someone to replace you, then they throw you out immediately, without pity and in the rudest possible manner.

Recently I had my fiftieth birthday. The previous day I was ordered to attend a meeting of the Party Bureau by Nikolai Yakovlevich Popov, the recently elected secretary and my former assistant. He made a crushing speech about me and tried to make an issue of my personal behavior. It turned out that I had not paid my union dues for a long time and that I had missed meetings of the philosophical society.

"You have completely broken your ties with the Party," he concluded his speech maliciously.

People are friendly to me in the faculty. I cannot complain about that. The final vote at the meeting was to forget about the matter. Happy Birthday.

# V. Science

I am very distressed by what is happening.

"Do you have enemies?" my imaginary accomplice asked.

"There are people who persecute me and wish for my downfall. Neither running away nor fighting back does any good. I don't know what to do."

"Be more specific."

"There is a group of highly placed mathematicians devoted, consciously and deliberately, to the expulsion of Jews from mathematics. They work in various ways and will use any means. The most scandalous, unprecedented, and dishonest is the practice of rejecting dissertations."

"What is this practice?"

"After a work has been defended at the Academic Council of a university or some other institution of higher education, it is sent to VAK, the Higher Certification Commission, for submission to expert opinion. A specially selected reader, popularly known as a "black reader," will write a negative report that recommends rejection even of work of high quality that fully deserves the degree. The Expert Committee then has a biased discussion, the outcome of which is predetermined, and votes to reject the work. All the participants in this practice know perfectly well that the dissertation has been rejected because, and only because, it is written by a Jew. This practice has existed for a long time, around seven years in fact. The number of candidate and doctoral dissertations rejected in this way is, by my calculations, well over a hundred and very likely several hundred."

"How did you get this information?"

"In the thick of battle. For almost two years I fought against the rejection of the candidate dissertation of my student B. His work is very good, far above average. I studied the elaborate mechanism of rejection and met people who had taken part in the rejection process and got to understand their motives. At the same time, I became acquainted with dozens of similar cases. Despite all my efforts, on December 22, 1976, VAK rejected the work that had been an integral part of my life for many years. Now it should be clear to you why I am so distressed by what is happening."

"You should lodge a protest. These people must be stopped. Do you know them?"

"I know many of them personally, and I know the names of the rest. All of them are either members of the Expert Committee, or members of the small group of experts who make up the narrow circle of readers. Because of the extent to which some of the cases are rigidly documented, an impartial investigation could easily be arranged. But will one ever take place? People have complained, but to no avail."

"What did they complain about?"

"The usual thing: A dissertation was rejected, but it was a good piece of work. There must have been a mistake. We request that the decision be reviewed and the dissertation confirmed."

"And the real reasons?"

"They are never mentioned: Nobody wants to get involved in politics."

"What has politics got to do with it? A specialist gives a deliberately false assessment of a dissertation and he votes to reject it on purely racial grounds. All this is against the law. These people, and if I understand you there are not many of them, should be exposed and punished or, at any rate, stopped from acting illegally. You must make a protest."

"Why me?"

"If not you, then who? How many times have you boasted that your striving for truth was the basis of your spiritual being. To prevent you from working in mathematics is to deprive you of the whole basis of your being. And then these people appear who deliberately distort the truth and who are knocking out from under you the foundations on which your life is built. Will you meekly submit? Are you afraid? Don't be afraid. You are already dead."

I wanted to reply but could not.

"Don't answer. I understand your feelings and your fears. Let us do it like this. You write out your protest in full, and then we will think about it."

## A Letter to the President of the Academy of Sciences

*Comrade President:*

You have only recently come to occupy your present high position. Now you are faced with the task of restoring justice.

I am referring to the need to destroy the militant anti-Semitism in our mathematics.

This phenomenon, which cultured people have always opposed, is all the more intolerable in our day when the "complete and final liquidation . . . of national oppression and racial discrimination . . . is the optimistic prospect which Communists hold out to the world." It is especially repulsive among scholars, the purpose of whose lives is the unceasing search for truth.

I am not referring, as is usual in such cases, to something formless and intangible. I give you concrete addresses: the Steklov Institute of Mathematics of the Soviet Academy of Sciences and the Expert Committees for Mathematics and Mechanics of VAK. I give you concrete people. I shall name only a few of the most active among them: Academician I. M. Vinogradov, Corresponding Members of the Soviet Academy of Sciences A. I. Shirshov, Yu. L. Ershov, S. V. Yablonskii, and Doctors of Physical and Mathematical Sciences A. A. Karatsuba and P. L. Ul'yanov. They are committing a crime against science, to say nothing of behaving in a way which is not only immoral but also punishable according to Soviet law and the Soviet constitution.

They are consciously and deliberately, and on a large scale, using the Expert Committees of VAK to reject good dissertations because their authors are Jewish. The matter has now gone beyond the bounds of decency. Dozens of doctoral dissertations have been rejected in this way, and many dozens of candidate dissertations. Perhaps an exact count would yield a number in the hundreds. This is unprecedented. There has been nothing like it in the whole history of science.

Things have gone so far that there is no longer any attempt to observe even the appearance of decency. Jews constitute two-thirds, three-quarters, and sometimes even 100 percent of those groups summoned by the Expert Committee to defend dissertations that have been rejected.

When you begin to investigate this matter, and you must do so for the sake of the future health of our science and society, you will discover a cesspool of scientific unprincipledness.

Readers give negative reports that are deliberately false and utterly biased and that ignore all the norms of scientific procedure. These reports are openly incompetent.

Committee meetings in fifteen or twenty minutes reject dissertations that represent the result of many years of difficult work and that have received the positive approval of many specialists as well as international recognition. In situations where there are conflicting viewpoints, a long and detailed analysis is required, with no restriction on time. Only in this way can there be a well-substantiated decision. Then it does not matter what issues are raised. It should not be the case, however, that participants in the discussion who themselves are not specialists in the field should be allowed to fight actively for a rejection while the real specialists are denied entrance into these meetings and are left standing outside the door when they insist on their right to express an opinion. Why? Because someone who knows the subject would only interfere.

Ambition has motivated people to cling insistently to odious decisions despite widespread general outrage. Examples can be found in the shameful decisions in the cases of the dissertations of Tsalenko and Vinberg, when they were submitted for reconsideration at the Steklov Institute.

All the members of the Expert Committee and all of the expert readers are responsible in varying degrees. Many simply submitted to pressure to avoid conflict and to hang on to their privileges. Remove this yoke from them and they will tell you immediately that they did not know, that they were forced against their will.

In conclusion:

I ACCUSE   Ivan Matveevich Vinogradov of being the chief organizer and the instigator of anti-Semitism in our mathematics. In his declining years let him consider how he will look in the mirror of history: an outstanding creator or the poisoner of the spirit of fair scientific enquiry?

I ACCUSE   Anatolii Alekseevich Karatsuba of rejecting, in opposition to practically the universal opinion of specialists, good and even brilliant work in number theory from motives of racial prejudice. May his sick conscience give him no rest!

I ACCUSE   Yurii Leonidovich Ershov and Anatolii Illarionovich Shirshov of having created an intolerable situation in the field of algebra by persecuting people who do not share their extreme views.

I ACCUSE   Petr Lavrent'evich Ul'yanov, who in his work on the Admissions Committee at Moscow University violated the norms of fair selection and was instrumental in the rejection of good dissertations at Moscow University and on the Expert Committee of VAK.

I ACCUSE   Sergei Vsevolodovich Yablonskii of introducing racial politics into mathematical cybernetics.

I ACCUSE   the Expert Committee of VAK in Mathematics and Mechanics of violating its responsibility by the frequent and deliberate rejection of dissertations by Jewish mathematicians that deserved to be confirmed.

I ACCUSE   the Institute of Mathematics of the Academy of Sciences of being dominated by a spirit of anti-Semitism and intolerance that is poisoning mathematical life.

You must intervene and make the situation healthy again. Do not be deterred by considerations of the honor of the great institution that you head. It will not suffer.

You must:
Totally replace the staff of the Expert Committee.
Pension off Vinogradov immediately.
Open wide the windows of the Steklov Institute. It stinks like a corpse.
The words with which a man of great spirit concluded his historical letter are also my words.
You must personify, as the head of Soviet scientists, the great principles of scientific honor and the striving for truth and justice. Thus will you fulfill your duty.
Be assured, Comrade President, of my deepest respect for you,
(signed) Grigori Freiman,
Professor and Doctor of Physical and Mathematical Sciences.

And now some more details.

## Ivan Matveevich Vinogradov

"Was born on 14 September (n.s.) 1891. His father, Matvei Avraam'evich, was a priest at the cemetery of Milolyub in the Velikoluk district of Pskov province.... His parents sent him to the technical school in the district town of Velikie Luki in 1903, to which his father moved from Milolyub with his family when he obtained a position at the Pokrovskii church."[1]
It is possible that as a result of his childhood impressions he developed a hatred of Jews—a hatred that has been one of the mainsprings motivating the activity of his energetic nature. His other basic passions are a thirst for power and a love of mathematics. As a mathematician he has been remarkable. That cannot be disputed.
I. M. Vinogradov has always spoken aloud of his attitude to

1. B. N. Delone, *The Petersburg School of Number Theory*, 1947, p. 321 (in Russian).

Jews, albeit behind peoples' backs. At the time N was defending his dissertation, he spent a lot of time at the Steklov Institute. He met Ivan Matveevich more than once. He testifies that when Vinogradov is in his office with two or three of his close friends, no matter how the conversation starts it is always channeled into the same course. With relish and enthusiasm they start to abuse Jews.

The Nemchinovs lived in an academic village and their *dacha* was next to Vinogradov's. He often saw the Nemchinovs over the fence, but he never approached them or said hello. And then one day he went up to Mrs. Nemchinova and said:

"Hello, Mariya Ivanovna. You know, I thought that you and Vasilii Sergeevich were Jews!"

Once, when Vinogradov received a telephone call from higher authority abusing Shafarevich, he answered:

"Shafarevich is not a Jew."

"Yes, but. . . ."

"He is not a Jew. I've checked that myself."

"Yes, but. . . ."

"Shafarevich is not a Jew, and other things about him don't concern me."

I think that this well-known anecdote has a certain basis in reality: Vinogradov took a dislike to Sabirov over something. He said, "Who is this Sabirov? Is he Shapiro?"

He always referred to my teacher, Aleksandr Osipovich Gel'fond, even to his face, as Sashka-Yid.

A fine administrator and politician, for several decades Vinogradov has held in his hands all the reins controlling mathematical life. Everything of real importance—electing new members of the Academy, awarding prizes, sending people abroad—is done according to his decision and under his control. Other mathematicians, no matter how famous they may be, have little voice. For example, Mark Grigor'evich Krein was nominated for the Lenin prize many years in succession. Finally, Aleksandrov, Kolmogorov, and Petrovskii published an article in *Izvestiya* insisting on the necessity of awarding Krein the prize, but to no avail.

When I found out that Karatsuba was preparing to reject *B*'s work, I decided to go and see Vinogradov—for the third time in my life.

I first met him in the summer of 1956 at the Third Mathematical Congress, where I delivered a paper. After my lecture he came over to me and said with approval, "Not bad." He paused for a moment and repeated, "Not bad, not bad. . . ." Then he left.

Our second meeting took place shortly before the defense of my doctoral dissertation at the beginning of 1965. I had been invited to the Steklov Institute and had been waiting for a long time on the second floor outside the director's office. Finally, Vinogradov appeared, his short, heavy, massive stooping figure and his large clean-shaven head bending forward, his arms hanging by the sides of his strong body almost to the floor. He looked just like an orangutan. We went into his office and I was given the royal treatment for over two hours. I presented Vinogradov all my work and talked about my results. He was very encouraging. Ivan Matveevich spoke unhurriedly. He digressed into the past, talked of all kinds of incidents and told anecdotes that imparted a zest to the conversation and allowed us time to think about more serious things.

I did not see him again. Knowing his antipathies, I did not try to meet him personally, even though we share the same area of scientific interest and I have drawn much from his work.

And so now, at this crucial moment, I decided to resort to him for help. After turning the whole thing over in my mind I rang him at his home, introduced myself and suggested that we meet to talk over some common scientific problems. I. M. recognized me immediately. He said he was ill and proposed a meeting when he felt better.

Three months later I went to see Konstantin Vasil'evich Borozdin, Vinogradov's personal assistant. He is not a mathematician, but a very intelligent person and a fine administrator. He always heard me out, and then carefully—even politely—explained why Vinogradov was not there, or that he was busy. He would then invite me to ring the following week. I had almost given up hope when Borozdin invited me to come on a Thursday for a meeting.

When I climbed the stairs that Thursday I bumped into three young Negroes, accompanied by the personnel officer.

"Vinogradov was just about to see you, but he is going to see the Negroes now." Borozdin spoke in his usual lapidary style, measuring his words. At this point he paused and added, "And the Arabs."

"In that case I will have to wait," I said.

Soon the Negroes proceeded into the office . . . but there were no Arabs, and I realized that this was simply a subtle joke on Borozdin's part.

I did not get to see Vinogradov that day, but I did get to see him on the following Tuesday.

The secretary politely invited me to sit in the large reception room, went into Vinogradov's office, and then called me in. Ivan Matveevich was enthroned behind a large writing table near the left hand wall, between two large windows. On the other side of the huge office hung a large board. When I entered, Ivan Matveevich got up, offered me his hand and invited me to sit in the chair at the right of the big table. The conversation unfolded slowly. Knowing his manner, I had expected that. So the finale was all the more unexpected. I reminded him of our last meeting and of my work in additive number theory. I informed him that I had managed to apply my ideas to probability theory. Vinogradov then began to develop his favorite topic—the relationship between form and content in mathematical research. This well-known controversy between two schools of mathematicians is described in Bourbaki's *The Architecture of Mathematics* as the opposition between the strategic approach (form) and the tactical approach (content). Which is more important—structure or results? I believe that results are more important and so did Vinogradov.

I decided to get to the point slowly.

"Lately I have been very interested in Markov's famous problem about arithmetical minima of quadratic forms, and I think I have achieved some fundamental results."

"Is that the problem, the one," Ivan Matveevich hesitated, "the one that Delone set?"

That sentence illuminated the whole situation like a bolt of lightning. It spoke volumes. This old man sat in his armchair self-assured and established. He spoke clearly. His large clean-shaven head, his broad figure, the unhurried movements of his large parted hands were as imposing as ever. I realized, however, that his mind was no longer powerful and his memory was slipping. It had become more difficult to dissemble.

He did not know which problem I meant. He must have known it at one time, but he had forgotten. This is what Delone wrote about that work of Markov: "This work, which was so highly regarded by Chebyshev, is among the finest accomplishments of the Petersburg school of number theory as well as of the whole of Russian mathematics.[2]

Vingradov, a representative of that school, had not recognized the famous problem of Markov in Delone's reference. Yet, he had been discussing it with someone. With whom? What exactly had they been discussing?

Then it was perfectly clear to me. It was precisely in Markov's problem that $B$ had made serious advances. Karatsuba had discussed $B$'s results with Vinogradov and had described his work as an advance in some insignificant problem set by Delone.

I already knew that nothing was too trivial for Ivan Matveevich. He kept every little thing under his control. Karatsuba must have received exact instructions from Vinogradov about $B$'s dissertation and the rejection of the work was according to his instructions.

I nodded vaguely in answer to his question and suggested, "If you don't object, I will briefly characterize the results."

Vinogradov nodded his agreement. I stood up and went over to the board.

"A lot of minima can be exhibited as points on a straight line, as points of a spectrum."

I drew a line on the board with a piece of chalk.

"Markov found all the points of the spectrum that are less than three. The next important result was by Marshall Hall, who proved that a ray enters the spectrum. What is its point of origin? B. N. Delone and his student proved that it lies to the left of 6.4. A

2. Ibid., p. 144.

student and I, and Hall as well, got an improvement to 5.1." (I took a breath before getting to the most important part.) "A very sharp improvement, with a new method, was obtained by *B*. His estimate was 5.04."

At that moment the secretary entered the room and approached Vinogradov. I was too absorbed in what I was saying to pay close attention, but later when I thought over what had happened I remembered that he told her tersely, "Sit down." She sat in the chair I had just occupied. I continued speaking.

"I was able to strengthen *B*'s result. I found the exact value of the source of Hall's ray. It turned out to be 4.52 when rounded off." With a triumphant look I chalked in this significant point on the line.

Suddenly the atmosphere in the office changed radically. The silence and calm disappeared. The door was flung open and shut. In fact, only two people entered the room—Borozdin and Mischenko, the deputy director—but it seemed as if a whole crowd had burst in. They opened some files and handed over some papers to Vinogradov for his signature. They crowded around the table, cutting me off from Ivan Matveevich, who had been so accessible before, with an impenetrable wall. I did not realize what was happening immediately, but instinctively realized that I should cut things short.

"I have covered the most important part," I said. I moved towards the desk. Ivan Matveevich's satelites circled around the table in a mute dance as if I were about to harm their beloved boss. They were willing to prevent my getting to him with their lives, if need be. I was just able to force my way through. I picked up my books, which I had put on the table at the beginning of the conversation, and gave them to Vinogradov indicating the passage on the significance of the source of the ray.

"I will look at it," Ivan Matveevich said. "You must excuse me."

And he made a gesture in the direction of the new arrivals and the papers awaiting his signature. As I headed for the door he rose from the table, a huge, massive hunched-over figure, and offered me his hand. I shook it, again barely managing to push through the close formation of his vassals. And—I retired from the battlefield.

Not until I was out in the corridor did I understand what had really happened. When he heard the name $B$, Vinogradov realized what I was leading to and furiously began pressing the button on his desk, calling all his assistants. They had prior instructions about what to do when the moment came to get rid of me.

## Anatolii Alekseevich Karatsuba

A long time ago I would meet Karatsuba at Gel'fond's seminars. As an undergraduate he specialized in number theory under Korobov and later became one of his graduate students.

He was well-proportioned, slim, and quite shy. He always wore a spotless white shirt and was extremely courteous. He was a keen mountain climber. He held the most progressive views.

$B$ was also Korobov's student at that time and a very close friend of Tolya (Karatsuba). For the first two years after Karatsuba had been working at the Steklov Institute the relationship remained unchanged. Whenever $B$ went to the Steklovka, Karatsuba was very friendly to him.

Karatsuba changed drastically after Ivan Matveevich drew him into his circle. He broke off with his old university friends and even stopped greeting them. At that time Vinogradov and Korobov were involved in a dispute over priority. Nikolai Mikhailovich Korobov was hounded out of the Institute, and Karatsuba assisted Vinogradov in every way possible. To this day Korobov is making the rounds of the departments seeking reinstatement.

Karatsuba emerged in his new role when Feinleib's doctoral dissertation was being defended at the Lenin Pedagogical Institute. The consensus of the specialists was that it was a good piece of work, certainly well up to the required standard. Karatsuba appeared at the defense to make a totally unfounded attack, and the work fell one vote short of the required two-thirds majority. To this day Feinlieb is not a doctor.

When $B$'s dissertation was being defended I did not worry for a moment about its chances. I did not consider getting additional references or organizing other support. Why should I? The dissertation was very good, and a good dissertation could not be rejected. I did not even worry when I discovered that Karatsuba was the expert who would review dissertations on number theory. What of it? He will try to find fault with it, but he does not make the decision alone. If the whole council of the best mathematicians judges the work on its merits, it would not be rejected.

As the review dragged on, however, we began to worry. I found out who the reader was. My information led me to the Steklovka and Dolbilin. I knew of Dolbilin. He was a young lad of about twenty-five who had recently defended his candidate's dissertation and now worked in Delone's department. Now I felt uneasy. Why should the work have been sent to a youngster who was not a specialist in the field?

I called Delone. He knew nothing but promised to make inquiries. That put me on my guard. Delone did not know that Dolbilin, who worked in his own department, had the dissertation? Dolbilin had not mentioned it to him, even though he had the dissertation in his possession for the last three months?

The second time I spoke to Delone on the telephone I caught the unmistakable odor of corruption with which I have lived so intimately for the last few years. Yes, Dolbilin has received the work for an opinion. He has only just received it, and that is why he has not had time to make a report. He does not like the work. It is very specialized. And he particularly does not like the fact that the conditions for the coincidence of the spectra of Markov and Lagrange are not obtained everywhere but only on certain intervals.

"But those conditions are necessary and sufficient, and that is a major advance," I objected.

Arguments of the kind put forward by Dolbilin are irrefutable. You may be the first to swim the English channel. That is not good enough because you did not swim across the Atlantic Ocean all the way to America.

Although Delone tries to avoid conflict, he always tells the truth when pressed for an opinion. He arranged a meeting for the following Thursday. He, Dolbilin, and I were to meet and get to the truth of the matter in the course of a scientific discussion. On the Wednesday I rang Delone to remind him of the meeting.

"Kolya Dolbilin has beaten us to it," said Boris Nikolaevich

Delone. "Today he sent the dissertation back to VAK without comment."

Slowly I began to comprehend the motives for such behavior. The carrot Ivan Matveevich dangled in front of Karatsuba was the title of corresponding member of the Academy of Sciences. What was in it for Dolbilin? The coming defense of his doctoral dissertation and the promise of an apartment. And so he took the job of "black reader" and danced to Karatsuba's tune. But he could not keep the thing a secret and realized that a scandal was looming. Delone had found out. M had telephoned him to ask for an explanation. If he sent in a negative report he would be disgraced and he was not ready for that. He still had not burned all his bridges the way Karatsuba had. If he sent a positive report he would lose his job. So he sent the dissertation back without comment.

Listen to the howl of the defenders of the "New Union of True Russian People in Mathematics": "The dissertation is weak—that is the reason for the rejection. All your subtleties are simply hallucinations. They never existed!"

But I have a witness. Dolbilin himself. Not long ago in conversation with a group of friends he gave his own, (and to his credit) true version of what happened. Yes, the work was very good. Not without flaws, but completely worthy of the degree. That is why he sent the work off without comment. The case is hopeless. The work will be rejected again because Vinogradov and Karatsuba hate the author's supervisor.

I have now lost track of the dissertation, nor do I know who Karatsuba has chosen as a reader.

I went to Delone. Boris Nikolaevich is the oldest of Soviet mathematicians. At 86 he is even one and a half years older than Vinogradov. The old man likes me, although irony and caustic remarks sprinkle his conversation like spice in eastern food. Since the death of his wife he has aged a great deal. His face has grown much thinner, he is losing his grey hair, and he has lost most of his teeth. Until recently he was like a young man. It was always pleasant to look at his bronzed, weather-beaten face. He would come to work at the Steklovka in a blue woollen training suit with white borders. He had been an outstanding mountain climber and a keen sportsman. Once, in winter, he casually asked me if he might open the ventilation window.

"All you Semites are afraid of fresh air," he said, as he climbed onto the window ledge and slammed open the window. He jumped back onto the floor, a bit heavily, but with great agility. He was very pleased with himself.

The old man had no desire to get involved in this skirmish. As usual I sat with him for several hours and he once again related all the events of his youth, all the Moscow mathematical anecdotes. I already knew that Pontryagin had written a negative report on a very good doctoral dissertation by Vinberg at Moscow University. Lev Semenovich Pontryagin is a mathematician whose achievements have already become classics. A strange line of thought, not unique to him, led him in later years to the conviction that Jewish mathematics was bad mathematics, and that it was his job to fight against it. It is said that for precisely this reason he insisted on scrapping the two-volume historical review, *Fifty Years of Mathematics in the Soviet Union*. This book never appeared in print.

"Vinberg came to me," Delone recounted, "and with tears in his eyes he showed me some ancient papers that proved that his grandfather had worked in an office of a tsarist government Ministry and held high rank. Thus he could not have been a Jew, and neither was he, Vinberg, a Jew. He was a russified Swede. I told this to Pontryagin when I met him and he muttered: 'Really?' and he seemed very disheartened.

When I met Vinberg and looked at him closely, I decided that he had turned down the honor of belonging to the chosen people in vain.

And so the conversation went on, until at last I could wait no longer and I asked him directly about *B*'s dissertation. If Boris Nikolaevich considered the dissertation to be weak, he should say so. But if the work was good, then he, as a pioneer in the field, should send an objective letter of recommendation. Delone thought for a while, then he took up a pen and wrote a positive report, which was sent to VAK.

In March of 1976, a negative report on the dissertation arrived from the reviewer at VAK. I will analyze this important document below in detail. Meanwhile I shall just say that it is a thoroughly spurious piece of paper. All this time, I had made no attempt to discuss the matter personally with Karatsuba. I had not considered for a moment that he was deliberately manipulating the reviewing process to get the dissertation rejected. But through some mutual acquaintances I received concrete information, taken from Karatsuba's own remarks, that clearly illustrated the hopelessness of the outcome.

At the end of March, when I was visiting *A*, I was advised to meet with Karatsuba anyway. No matter how clear indirect evidence made his position, it was necessary to confront him personally.

I happened to have at hand the telephone number of Karatsuba's wife (they do not exactly live together, nor are they completely separated). I telephoned and Karatsuba unexpectedly turned out to be there. When I introduced myself he was stunned and did not know what to say.

"I don't know much about the affair," he said finally. "I have not received the reader's report on the dissertation. When I get it we can arrange a meeting."

I rang him a week later and received the same answer. And a week after that the same. I realized that he was behaving like a timid mouse that assiduously burrows under the floor but is afraid to stick his nose out into the open. I did not manage to see him right up to the meeting of the Expert Committee, where the case was presented as a *fait accompli*.

After the rejection of the dissertation, and after I had made an appeal and the case had been returned to the expert committee, I rang him once again and discovered that Karatsuba had a "twinge of conscience." I was astonished at the depth of genuine human feeling he injected into the conversation on this occasion.

"Anatolii Alekseevich, we must arrange a meeting to discuss the matter of *B*'s dissertation."

"Do you think so?"

And in his voice was an unbelievably vivid emotion of intense suffering.

I remained silent, waiting for a concrete answer. All of his words are authentic—I wrote them down directly after the conversation.

"I don't know . . ." his voice lowered almost to a whisper. He hesitated in great uncertainty, and his agreement came out painfully indefinite.

"When then?"

"Whenever you say," I said.

He whispered something (yes . . . yes . . . as if he were sorting something out to himself).

Then he became completely silent.

I waited. Nothing. Silence. I had to break it.

"We still have to talk."

He, in an embarrassed voice. "I understand."

Again a pause. At length he resumed his normal voice: "The thing is I am going abroad, that is the problem."

We arranged to meet when he returned.

After that conversation I decided not to telephone him any more.

But we did actually meet and have our talk not long before the final meeting of the Expert Committee, in which Karatsuba did his utmost to ensure the rejection of the dissertation.

The meeting took place by chance on a trolleybus. I knew that Karatsuba's wife lived in the building across from me, but I had never once met him close to the house. On this occasion I happened to get on a bus on Vernadskii Prospect and had sat down on a bench when I noticed that Karatsuba was sitting opposite me. We saw each other at once and looked each other in the eye, he somewhat hesitantly—many people now simply do not greet him. I nodded and he did the same and we looked away at the same time.

But could I leave without even saying a word? No, I have nothing to hide and nothing to be ashamed of. I must start a conversation and try for at least some semblance of normality. If, as in the case of Vinogradov, it all turns out to be in vain, at least I would have reached an understanding based on personal contact.

"Anatolii Alekseevich, since we have met we ought to have a talk about *B*'s dissertation."

"Yes, I remember it," said Karatsuba. "He was a student at Moscow University, I think."

How do you like that! If he met his own mother, this man would say, "I do believe we've met somewhere."

The trolleybus came to a stop, and we got out and began to walk along the sidewalk. There were about a hundred and fifty meters to his building, and I had to get to the point quickly.

"I know the dissertation very well. It is work of a very high caliber."

"But the reader made some criticism of the work. It contains some errors," Karatsuba started to recall.

"The report is not objective. There are no substantial errors in the work. The dissertation is very good. But that is not what I wish to discuss. (You yourself know that very well.) I am turning to you with a personal request. Do not attack the dissertation. You are the key man in any decision over its fate."

"What do you mean?" he said, defensively.

"No, that is a fact," I interrupted him. "Perhaps you and I have not seen eye to eye in the past, but that is not important."

"We have had no problems," Karatsuba said supportively.

"All the more reason to approve the work. It is the extremely successful result of many years of hard work."

"But the reader pointed out some errors, as I recall," Karatsuba repeated, with renewed interest and insistence in his voice.

No doubt the reader, and perhaps Karatsuba himself, had spent a considerable amount of time trying to find some faults in a carefully put together work, and Karatsuba wanted to know my opinion of his efforts.

"Yes, an error was pointed out. It is in no way substantial and can be corrected with the stroke of a pen. The remainder of the reader's remarks are simply mistaken."

Karatsuba said something vague. We exchanged the last handshake of our lives and parted.

I had wasted my words and humiliated myself for nothing. He could not afford to neglect a job given him by Vinogradov, especially on the threshold of the elections to the Academy of Sciences. But, given all of that, he still constantly sought to play down his participation in the whole dirty business.

At the committee meeting in December where he succeeded in

burying the dissertation once and for all, he sat self-effacingly with his hands on his knees. He did not once look at *B*, even when asking him questions.

## We do not like him

Vinogradov's and Karatsuba's attitude toward me, about which Dolbilin spoke, was not based on anything specific. I have already described my pleasantest meetings with Vinogradov, and I had likewise had no conflicts with Karatsuba apart from one small exception.

In 1971, an international conference on number theory took place in honor of the eightieth birthday of I. M. Vinogradov. I was not invited to that conference, and not because I was unqualified, since my students and graduate students received invitations. Levin and Pyatetskii-Shapiro were not invited, nor even Gel'fand. Erdös and Turán were not there.[3]

Karatsuba was the vice-chairman of the organizing committee. I went along to one of their meetings and met him in the corridor. In a querulous tone I told him of my grievances.

"It is too late now to do anything," Karatsuba said. "Go along to the meeting and take part in the work and I will tell them to let you through."

"But why is it really too late?" I asked insolently. "In my view it is a mistake which can quite easily be rectified." But he did not reply.

Apropos. Let me tell you something about contemporary conferences. The principles on which many of them are organized perfectly illustrate the extent of the demarcations in the mathematical world on the Jewish problem.

This spring in Georgia a conference was held on discrete programming. It was organized by A. Fridman. It turned out that Yablonskii organized a parallel conference on pure "Russian" cybernetics to which Jews were not invited. Moreover, Russians who associated with Jews were not invited. The principles of racial

3. These five mathematicians are Jewish. The first three are Soviet, the last two Hungarian.—Ed.

purity were also strictly observed at the conference on group thè-ory organized by Gorchakov in Krasnodar in 1976.

The Kishinev conference on mathematical logic. The abstracts had already been published. Shain had even received a letter in which he was urged to send off a correction to his paper. Suddenly a number of those who had been invited received notification that as a result of the large number of applications and the small number of hotel rooms available, it had been found necessary to withdraw their invitations. Among those who received rejections were Shain, Grindlinger, and Shneerson. Soon it became known what had happened behind the scenes in this affair. The members of the organizing committee, S. I. Adyan, Yu. L. Ershov, and S. V. Yablonskii, insisted the secretary of the organizing committee come to Moscow with the list of invited participants, and they then purged the list.

When he received his rejection, Shain sent a letter to Kishinev in which he remarked that the people who had been refused permission to participate had only one thing in common. It reminded him of the incident that took place in 1934 with Issai Schur, who received a letter from the *Deutsche Mathematische Vereinigung* in which his application to participate in a conference was rejected on the grounds that he had not reserved a hotel room early enough.

Whether as a result of this letter or for some other reason, all the original invitations were soon confirmed.

Adyan, Ershov, and Yablonskii did not go to Kishinev.

To help you understand my melancholy mood of isolation and loneliness, I shall describe my "trip" to Hungary. In the summer of 1973, a conference was to be held in Hungary in honor of the sixtieth birthday of Paul Erdös. Erdös' scientific interests were extremely close to my own. I got to know him well by meeting him on a number of occasions when he came to Moscow to take part in the International Congress of Mathematicians in 1966.

On that occasion I presented him with a copy of my book. As he was looking through it while we walked, he joked:

"It is a very good book."

"What do you mean?"

"By definition, a good book is one in which you are quoted."

I was sent an invitation to the Hungarian conference. I did not receive it, but I knew that it existed when I read the New Year greeting of Szemeredi, who finished with the words "until we meet in the summer in Balaton."

In my reply I asked him to send the invitation to my address at work. Not long after that, the secretary of the faculty party bureau handed me an envelope, which had been unsealed, containing the invitation.

I went to the rector.

Komin answered me right away that he had nothing against my trip, but that to send me he would have to receive instructions from above.

I went to the Ministry of Higher Education of the Russian Republic. There the Department of International Relations had received an order describing the procedure for my impending departure. The institute should vouch for me, the Ministry would enter the trip in its annual plan, the plan would be approved, and I could go. I went back to the rector, and thought that, after I explained the procedure, he would show some enthusiasm and make out my documents.

Nothing of the kind. He needed a directive from above. One more turn of the wheel. From the Ministry to the rector and now back again.

I went to the office of the Central Committee of the Communist party. There was a long line. Most of the people, to judge from their conversations, were newcomers with housing or work problems, or various legal difficulties. I found the telephone number of the Department of Science, called them, and explained that I wanted to see someone regarding an official trip abroad. A woman's voice gave me a telephone number. Someone answered the phone. I gave him the gist of my problem; he asked my name and where I worked, who I had spoken to in the Ministry, etc. Then he said in a very polite, even, clear, and business-like voice:

"I think that with this particular matter there is no point in your coming to see us. See the deputy head of the Department of International Relations at the Ministry of Higher Education." (He gave me the name.) "The head is not there, he is on vacation. Call such and such a number. They will see you and answer your questions." I thanked him and hung up. I went to the Ministry (on Zhdanov street), found the deputy, and stated my business. He was a very sympathetic young man, seated at a large table in an open office. I told him that the theme of the conference was of great interest to me, and that there would be no expense since the organizers had promised to pay for everything.

*Deputy*: "We make out the travel plan in March, and we have plenty of time to include you. If we receive a reference from your Institute in good time, there should be no problem."

*Me*: "That is precisely the problem. The Institute will not give me a reference until they get a directive from above."

*Deputy*: "How can we give you a directive without any information about you?"

*Me*: "I can see no sense in going around in circles. As I understand it, you are authorized to *make a decision*."

*Deputy*: "Go to Dubrovina, the deputy head of the Department of Universities on Leninskii Prospect.

*Me*: (impatiently) "But listen. You are just sending me lower down the ladder and I need someone who can make a decision."

*Deputy*: (decisively) "Go to Dubrovina. She is qualified to answer your questions."

I went to Dubrovina and was charmed by her pleasant, simple, and polite manner. My question did not present any difficulty.

"Komin, your rector, has not been with us for very long, and he does not yet know how we do things. We have a lot of people who travel abroad. I will telephone tomorrow and arrange for your journey."

She did not let me go immediately. She asked about my work, my methods of teaching, about Kalinin University. In short, an extremely pleasant conversation, but then they so often are.

I let a day go by to be safe, then I went to the rector's office. Dubrovina still had not called. I called her immediately from the rector's office and reminded her of me. This time her voice was not as affable. She was short and businesslike.

"I will ring Komin right away," she said.

I walked around for a good half hour in the corridor. When I went back to the office, I was told there had been a conversation between the rector and Dubrovina and I went into the rector's office.

"Vladimir Vasil'evich, you asked me for a directive from above," I said with an air of assurance. "Now you have it. I assume everything is in order?"

"What do you mean?" Komin asked.

"Well, Dubrovina has just spoken with you," I said half questioningly. What Komin said knocked me completely off balance.

"Yes, I have spoken to Dubrovina. What about it? That conversation means nothing. I must have a *directive*. Then I will be able to authorize your journey."

"And that conversation is not such a directive?" I asked, puzzled as to what this mysterious directive might be and how I could get hold of one.

"No, it is not."

At this time I realized (about time?) that the whole matter had already been decided. Later I was told what the rector had said. "What would happen to us if we let Freiman go to Hungary, Ryzhak go to Japan, and Freiburg go to Yugoslavia?"

And so nobody went anywhere.

## The negative report

The reader's comments on B's dissertation were sent to B by mail. We prepared a reply together and spent about two weeks on it. We made it very convincing and well substantiated. It was only later, with shock and amazement, that I found out that it was never read. The reply was not looked at by a single soul.

I have the reader's report and our reply in front of me as I write. My thoughts all lead me to one conclusion. We submitted naïvely to the rules of mathematical debate and only tried to make it clear that the reader's allegations were wrong or mistaken. In fact this was not the root of the matter at all. The reader was simply dishonest. He was a cheat and a liar.

The anonymous author of the report, let us call him *S*,[4] made up his report with the fully conscious intention of discrediting an extremely significant and extremely thorough work. Because of this report, he deserves to be excluded from the community of scientists. But who can prove it? Mathematical material is not meant for light reading. The number of specialists in the whole world who can grasp the essence of the mathematical problem immediately is very small. Other mathematicians cannot spare the time. One good thing, at least, is that mathematical assertions are durable and do not allow for ambiguity. Mathematical truth is completely unequivocal. I am not making unsubstantiated statements. I place on the scales all the baggage I have acquired in a lifetime of work and my irreproachable scientific reputation and the truth of what I say will be valid even in a hundred years.

Meanwhile, listen in to the dialogue.

*Reader*: "All of these signs give us nothing new in terms of effectiveness in comparison with the definition."

*Me*: "The definitions are not effective, the signs are."

*Reader*: "He only proves the existence of two very small intervals."

*Me*: "The reader is continually using derogatory adjectives with the intention of creating a psychological background for rejecting the work—'some very small,' 'a very particular character,' 'a whole series of errors,' 'an insignificant advance.' In this particular instance the intervals discovered are indeed very small. But is that really bad? And what can be done if large intervals with the given necessary properties do not exist? Try to reproach a physicist for the fact that the new element which he has discovered is 'very small.'"

*Reader*: "The dissertation abounds in errors and misprints."

*Me*: "An analysis of the reader's comments shows that he has only indicated one error, which can easily be eliminated (and in fact was eliminated in two lines in the text of the reply), and a few misprints. The work was written and put together with great care."

---

4. I have in my possession impressive evidence that the last name really does begin with an *S*.

*Reader*: "On the whole the entire dissertation has a purely computational character, and has no theoretical value whatsoever."

*Me*: "The entire work has a purely theoretical character; only section 15 is devoted to calculations. In his work $B$ has developed a new method of investigating the Hall ray.[5] The work has great theoretical significance and has already achieved recognition both here and abroad."

The discussion could be continued. The assertions of the disputants are diametrically opposed. I will answer for my assertions and I am ready to defend them in any public dispute.

Such dishonest false reports are not unique. They can be counted already in the hundreds. How did it ever come about that mathematics, the most honest of sciences, became so rotten?

## Sergei Ivanovich Adyan

I telephoned Adyan the day after the meeting of the Expert Committee, which he attended, at which $B$'s dissertation was turned down.

"Sergei Ivanovich?"

"Yes, what can I do for you?" His voice on the telephone was soft and intelligent.

"This is Freiman speaking. You probably know of me. I believe Andrei Andreevich has mentioned me."

No, he did not quite remember me. That, to say the least, was simply not so. Only the day before he personally mentioned my name several times.

"I work on number theory, but a lot of my work is related to algebra. I would like to present you with my books and also discuss the problem of $B$'s dissertation, which is threatened with rejection."

"But I am just going to a meeting."

"It doesn't necessarily have to be right away. When would you be free?"

"I am usually in the Steklov Institute at two o'clock in the afternoon."

5. This sentence is taken from Delone's report. Everything else is taken from the reader's report and our reply to it.

"Good. I will come along at that time."

"Well"—his voice showed no enthusiasm for the impending meeting—"I might happen to be somewhere else when you come. You had better telephone me at two, just to check."

"Even better, I will ring you early in the morning so as to arrange a precise time."

"Very well," he said, and he decided to forestall the possibility of an unpleasant conversation. "If it were not for the business of B you would probably not have called me?"

"Possibly not," I agreed. "However, it is a convenient stimulus for us to get together. I will be able to tell you about my work as well as the work of B, which is of a very high caliber."

"I am not a specialist in number theory, and I am not very well acquainted with its results, but yesterday I had a talk with him and he seemed very unconvincing. The impression he produced was very confusing."

"Oh, yes. Well, I have been concerned with this topic for many years and I know it well."

"Yes, I have heard. You have obtained some positive results."

"So, I will be able to explain to you clearly and lucidly about B's work, which, I repeat, is of a very high caliber." I underlined the last words expressively.

"But it contains mistakes?"

"Some defects do exist, but they are not of any substance."

"Well, you see"—his voice sounded a little more confident, but he was still not very certain—"as a supervisor, I always take the responsibility upon myself to ensure the work is accurately written up."

"Well, until tomorrow then," I said, to finish the conversation. If only he knew how much work I had put into checking the writing of that dissertation.

The next day I went to the Steklovka and found Adyan's office. He politely invited me in, sat down by the window, and asked me to sit alongside him. He was of average height, with a dark, intelligent, and expressive face. His whole manner inspired sympathy and I found myself succumbing to his charm and his obvious attempt to make a good impression. Only later did I begin to compare critically his words with his previous behavior and to fathom their hidden meaning.

But at the time I found him very charming. He behaved quite unaffectedly, listened attentively to all I said. He did not try to brush aside rational arguments, but made an effort to understand them. I began by presenting him with my books, showed him an American translation of one of them; in short, I gave him my credentials. When I had showed him the book *The Markov Problem* I moved straight on to *B*'s work.

"I consider his work to be excellent, and the decision taken to reject it is the crudest error. I will never be reconciled to it. But before I substantiate that opinion, I want to back it with some general observations. I have worked on this problem for many years and I have obtained a number of quite substantial results. Therefore, I think I can judge the level and importance of his work. I categorically state that the dissertation is a sound piece of work, that the negative report was made by a man who is incompetent and dishonest, and the rejection of the work is an act of ignorance and deceit."

I continued talking and without noticing I began to raise my voice. All the accumulated bitterness of the previous sleepless nights came out, and my speech became more accusatory: "prejudice," "unjust," "amoral behavior" and "unprincipled acts" and some even more energetic and definite words crept out.

Adyan then made a very sudden unmistakable gesture, and said something like:

"Come on now, there is no need to get angry. That won't help matters." And he immediately led me back to the normal course of the conversation.

This is typical of the extremely paradoxical situation of our times. Nothing is actually carried on in the open. Previously when the shout "Beat the yids!" was heard, at least it was possible to cry for help and prepare to defend oneself. Now, however, even with the best-intentioned of people, I have to talk in Aesopian language. We both have to pretend we are discussing a purely scientific topic, whereas the real heart of the matter, which is on both our minds, is never confronted directly.

"I understand your conviction," said Adyan. "But you see a lot depends on the defense. The work may be very good but, when defending his arguments, he gets confused and his explanations are inconsistent. Moreover, he cannot explain intelligently the significance of his work. Consequently it is rejected. I see nothing wrong in that. He can defend it a second time and there is no stigma attached. I know of such cases. Your student, though, talked somewhat badly and unconvincingly."

I brushed aside his fallacious arguments with a dissatisfied gesture.

"What are you talking about a second defense! A dissertation, any dissertation, but this one in particular, is the result of many years of hard work. A multitude of problems have had to be overcome: getting it into polished form, publications, the organization of the defense. As for talking sensibly, he would talk very sensibly if you gave him the chance, instead of interrupting him and confusing him."

An incident, which is not out of place here, comes to my mind. It took place outside the office of the Committee. A group of people summoned to the defense of their work were waiting in line outside the room of the Expert Committee. One of them, from one of the Central Asian republics, shaking his head and puffing up his cheeks in ecstacy, said of Adyan:

"Wow! that Adyan, he is the titan of mathematics!"

The majority of those called to the so-called defense of their work do not have any idea what is in store for them. They become flustered and confused when they experience the hostile mood, the continual interruptions and digressions, and the deliberate attempt to bewilder them with authorities. And if this does not work and the defendant does not get confused, the outcome is just the same, only the defendant is accused of self-conceit (Shain, Levin).

I continued, "Let me tell you the theme and the results of *B*'s work." I got up, went over the board, took a piece of chalk, and began talking. Adyan listened carefully, asked a few questions, while I gave him the definitions. I drew a line on the board, placed the points on it, in short told him exactly what I had told Vinogradov at our meeting.

And then I began to realize one crucial point. Adyan knew essentially nothing about the problem. He did not even know the basic definitions.

This does not only apply to Adyan. It is also an indication of the level of work at the Expert Committee, which, as a rule, bases its judgments on the opinions of two or three of their members who are a lot closer to the subject matter of the work in question. (In our case these were Karatsuba, Andrianov, Kostrikin, and Adyan.) But these last did not acquaint themselves with the work beforehand. They looked through it on the spot, turning over pages during the meeting (that is what they did in our case), picking out particular sentences at random from the dissertation and the reader's report. In short, the backbone of the specialist committees relies on the expert—in our case the absent Karatsuba—and the reader, and no one ever gets to judge the work on its merits.

In my subsequent conversations with Kostrikin and Andrianov this suspicion was confirmed. They knew nothing of the Markov problem, either. Kostrikin hadn't got a clue, and Andrianov had only the vaguest idea.

Thus narrow specialists make a judgment and the remainder of the committee believes them. If these one or two specialists, in disregard of professional ethics, give false opinions in order to pursue their own egotistical ends, how can the poor committee make a proper decision?

In fact everyone taking part in this activity knows perfectly well how things stand. A lot can be understood simply from the testimony of the defendants themselves. And the flood of protests from specialists who, as a rule, are far more competent than the reviewers chosen by VAK. On top of that, the very fact that one after another, day after day, they see a constant stream of authors of "inferior" dissertations who are all Jewish—what does this say about those "honest, decent people,"[6] Adyan, Kostrikin, and Andrianov?

Let us return, however, to the description of my meeting with

6. This is the oral opinion of some well-known mathematicians who are not familiar with the activities of the people I have named on the Expert Committee.

Adyan. I was still standing at the board explaining the essence of the problem and the results.

"I will briefly try and explain the significance of what *B* accomplished in the second chapter of his dissertation," I said. "He obtained an estimate of 5.04 for the source of the Hall ray, and this was an improvement of five hundredths. Now if two American mathematicians, Hall and Bumby, expended much effort and could only advance by fractions of a thousand, then an improvement in terms of fractions of a hundred calls for undoubted recognition as a significant creative achievement. In this, as in other things, everything depends on the scale."

Adyan nodded, indicating he understood.

"Now you understand the unscrupulousness of the report. It contains five pages, and it mentions various things. But how does he deal with this most important result? In one phrase: In the second chapter he obtained an insignificant *improvement* in the estimate of the source of the ray."

Adyan picked up the report and began to look through it while I showed him the corresponding phrase.

"But that was not all. All other researchers who improved the estimate have used the original work of Hall, who used a method that is finally exhausted. *B* introduced new ideas and made a breakthrough. Building on that, I completed the solution of the problem. In the report there is not a word of all this. What can the report be worth after that? And how do you like the phrase: 'The whole work has a totally computational character and has no theoretical value.' That is simply a lie, evident to anyone who wants to examine it."

Adyan held the report and our reply in his hands, comparing them and working out the justice of my remarks.

It was clear that none of them had seen the reply. He was holding it in his hands for the first time.

I moved away from the board and back to my chair.

"I won't even explain the results of the first chapter. I will merely say that *K*, in his doctoral dissertation, gave sufficient conditions for the coincidence of the spectra of Markov and Lagrange, whereas *B* gave necessary and sufficient conditions."

"But *K* obtained his results earlier."

I brought out the article of Cusick.

"Look at this: '*K* has given many simple conditions that are sufficient to ensure that a given number in **M** [the Markov spectrum] is also in **L** [the Lagrange spectrum]. *B* has studied the more difficult problem of giving conditions that are sufficient to ensure that a given number is in **L**. In fact, for certain intervals on the real line, *B*'s conditions are both necessary and sufficient.'"

"And who is this Cusick?" asked Adyan.

"He is an American professor, a mathematician."

"And is he very well known? Of late it has become fashionable to give references from foreign publications, but any graduate student can throw quotations around. *K* still obtained his results earlier."

And we continued the dialogue in this way, like a game of billiards.

"But *K* received a doctorate and *B* is not even a Candidate of Sciences. And *K* himself highly regarded *B*'s work," I said. Adyan offered no objection.

"Well, what now? I have understood the significance of *B*'s results."

Only a lot later on did I understand what guided Adyan in his actions and words. He did what he was told. He had too much at stake to disobey: his career, influence. But now that the business was all over with and he was clear of the affair, he needed to justify himself as best he could and produce the best impression.

"It is a pity that you did nòt talk to me about all this before," he said to me reproachfully.

"But Andrei Andreevich Markov had already spoken to you," I objected.

"He is not a specialist and neither am I." (And Delone's report, and our reply to the reader, which made mincemeat of his arguments? Were they not at least worth looking at?)

Had he wanted he would have listened to Markov, the more so since the latter specifically tried to inform him of the opinion of specialists. Since he clearly had no desire to know, he would not have listened to me either, and even if he had, it would have had no influence on the outcome.

He came up with another rationale.

"Tell me, in the committee where the dissertation was defended, were there many specialists who understood the essence of the problem?"

"No, of course not. As always, only the supervisor and the readers, and perhaps two or three other people, knew the essence of the problem."

"There you see," said Adyan, settling on my words as if they offered him granite support. "Although Karatsuba was not present, he had left behind for us his conclusions. We also had the reader's report. Our negative conclusion was thus quite natural."

I got up at this point and furiously rejected his whole argument.

"I do not at all see the analogy in what you have just said. The committee does indeed often take decisions based on the positive comments of a few specialists, in the absence of any negative opinion and in an atmosphere of unanimity. But here we had a totally different situation. You turned down a work in a situation where there were conflicting points of view, and if you voted for a rejection you have taken upon yourself such a great responsibility that you are obligated to understand the merits of the case."

What difference did it make? One way or another the work had been rejected. Adyan gave me some hints in the course of our conversation. I found out who was on the committee. Vladimirov (chairman), Gonchar (deputy chairman), Andrianov, Bol'shev, Ershov, Millionshchikov, Samarskii, Poznyak, Ul'yanov, Yablonskii.

In the course of further conversation, we energetically discussed how to get the work confirmed. When I told him I wanted to see all those who had taken part in this rejection, I became incensed once more at the memory of what had taken place. Almost in passing he said to me:

"You yourself, what do you really want? To get the dissertation confirmed or to create a scandal?"

I answered without considering the underlying meaning of his question.

"I will do all I can to get the dissertation confirmed, but if any injustice takes place I shall raise a scandal."

We had been sitting for two hours. Our conversation had started to touch more trivial subjects, and was beginning to fragment. I got up abruptly, wishing to leave, and said goodbye.

"Where are you going? Sit a while longer," Adyan said.

"I am happy to sit and talk as long as you want, but I did not want to keep you." And I sat down surprised and touched by his concern.

Our conversation continued on the friendliest of notes. Sergei Ivanovich expressed sympathy with all of my plans, and I soon began to warm towards him, despite my earlier restraint.

Nonetheless, as I was about to leave, I ventured to give him my principled opinion of the matter.

"All the same, Sergei Ivanovich, I must say that you personally committed a grave error in voting against *B*'s work, and I cannot excuse you from responsibility for your fundamentally incorrect behavior." It was too late now to change the trusting, friendly tone of the conversation. Although Adyan raised no objection, the expression on his face changed considerably.

I left, but once in the reception room, I discovered I had left my umbrella behind. I went back to Adyan's room, apologized, retrieved my umbrella. Adyan was sitting perfectly still, looking very morose. He looked at me somewhat distantly but did not speak or stir an inch.

## Aleksei Ivanovich Kostrikin and Anatolii Nikolaevich Andrianov

Kostrikin and Andrianov can be dealt with in less space. They are of the same ilk as Adyan.

*K*, who is one of the leading Soviet mathematicians, is distinguished, among other things, for the independence and forthrightness of his opinions.

"The report is repulsive and its author is simply dishonest," he said when he heard about the reopening of the case. Thinking about whom he could turn to for help, *K* said, "I will talk with Kostrikin. Aleksei Ivanovich will not turn you down."

The next day he telephoned me and said:

"Aleksei Ivanovich surprised me very much. He refuses to meet you. I tried to discuss the dissertation with him, but he claims that it is purely computational work. I told him that is simply not true and that it would be worth his while to discuss it with you, since you could explain it better than anyone. But he sees no need for that. He says he understands already."

A meeting did take place, however, in Kyarieku, at a symposium on the theory of rings and modules. The symposium was held at the sports center of Tartu University. Here in the lap of nature I met Kostrikin face to face. I introduced myself and asked when he would be free for a talk.

"Why delay? There is no time like the present," he said, as if he were talking of having a tooth pulled.

The conversation was surprisingly short. I described the problem. Kostrikin asked a few questions. I told him enthusiastically why the work was good.

"Well then," he said, having heard me out. "I will put in a good word for it if I can."

He got up and I said goodbye, feeling there was no point in talking. He himself obviously did not understand the discrepancy between his behavior and his words. Why did he not try to put me off with the version that the dissertation was purely computational? Because he knew that nonsense would not wash with me as I was thoroughly acquainted with the work. Why did he not continue to abuse the work if he sincerely considered it to be bad? And even if he had changed his opinion, he should have been very concerned; something very exceptional had happened. A scientist had mistakenly obstructed a good dissertation. Neither was, in fact, the case. He had promised to put in a good word when he really meant that he would buy a good pair of imported boots.

In December he was elected a Corresponding Member of the Academy of Sciences. That event was closely related, as Ivan Matveevich Vinogradov confesses, to his work on the Expert Committee.

When I spoke to M, who is closely linked by his scientific interests with Anatolii Nikolaevich Andrianov, he said that *all that* has upset him very much. He skips meetings so as to avoid *all that*. When I met Andrianov in the Leningrad section of the Steklov Institute, we had a very forthright conversation. We discussed how to put matters to rights. He spoke of his desire to help. That platonic desire, however, was limited by an opposing and almost imperative desire to render aid in the least noticeable way and with a minimum of conflict. I did not have to spend much time proving to Andrianov that *B*'s dissertation was good. He expressed himself with the utmost clarity:

"I'm afraid I was defending Kirshtein's dissertation. As a result, I was not able to do anything in your case."

He promised that when the work came up for a second review he would find a second, unbiased reader. He probably would have fulfilled his promise but Karatsuba was at the meeting and attacked the work energetically. Andrianov would not enter into a conflict and the dissertation was rejected again.

What is there to say? If you have successfully defended a good dissertation by Kirshtein, you do not have to attack another good work . . . and yet Andrianov is a good mathematician and a well-known scientist. International contacts are very important for him. A couple of years ago he went to the States. In January he went to France for three months. If he created a scandal or expressed his opinion clearly and categorically he would not be sent anywhere nor allowed to accept invitations.

If that trio knew my opinion they would be very offended: they voted against *B*'s dissertation because they were forced to. And if they could have helped they would have done so because they were sympathetic. Why should they be abused? I would advise them to read the letters of Thomas Mann to Rudolf and Hans Friedrich Blunck.[7]

---

7. Translations of these letters appear in *Letters of Thomas Mann 1889–1955*, trans. Richard Winston and Clara Winston (New York: Alfred A. Knopf, Inc., 1971), 485–86, 505–7.—Ed.

## To the Toilers of the Expert Committee!

On 21 May 1976 a special extraordinary meeting of the Expert Committee was called. As always, it was held in the Steklov Institute, where the majority of the committee members work. By five o'clock all those summoned were in the conference hall. The noise of a crowd of people talking in undertones filled the corridors outside the committee room. About 100 people had gathered. This was a large assembly. Normally only a dozen or so degree defendants were summoned, but this time, because of the need to finish the affairs of the old VAK and of the approaching summer vacation, it was decided to hold a general purge.

The national composition of the assembled people was striking and immediately noticeable. They were either Jews or members of the eastern republics: Turkmens, Tadjiks or Azerbaijanis. This impression was confirmed when the secretary began to call out the surnames to check on the attendance: Kirshtein, Mukhitdinov, Vassenmakher, Niyazbekov, etc. There was not a single Russian name. Of the hundred or so people there, over *half* were Jewish— some 60 people.

Everyone was organized into sections. This was a clear breach of regulations, for every case is supposed to be heard by the full committee, and it is certainly not allowed to rubber stamp a hundred rejections in one evening. In the section for algebra, number theory, and mathematical logic there were eight people—five Jews and three people from Central Asia.

The committee began work at seven o'clock and continued until eleven. Everyone had been told to arrive at five, however, and since the names were called out randomly they all had to wait outside the door the whole time. There was not a single chair. The whole crowd, many of whom had come directly from the train, had to stand for hours.

In the rest breaks for the committee members a special room was reserved for tea and sandwiches. Meanwhile, in the corridor between the door behind which the "toilers" of the Expert Committee were busy and the refectory, an atmosphere of camaraderie, almost of brotherhood, sprang up. Everyone was using the familiar form of address and there was much back-slapping, joking, and laughing. Soon it was a tightly knit group.

Finally it was time to discuss $B$'s dissertation. The committee held a preliminary discussion, but the door was slightly ajar, and in the corridor we heard a loud burst of laughter when Delone's report was read. To other people that may not mean very much. It spoke volumes to me. It meant that now the reins were firmly in the hands of young people who, in their self-assurance, had consigned the once-eminent names of Aleksandrov, Markov, Kolmogorov, and Delone to the receding mists of time. Those old men, the bearers of these names, were no more than ghostly shadows. If they attempted to intervene in decisions of the real world they were simply laughed at. That burst of laughter told me one thing more: the rejection of the dissertation was now a foregone conclusion.

At last they called $B$ in.

I went into a long room. On the left by the wall was a table behind which Andrianov and Adyan were sitting. Opposite them was a board and a chair for my use. At a separate table Kostrikin sat with his back to the window. There were three more people in the room but they did not take part in the discussion. The people responsible for rejecting the dissertation were Adyan, Andrianov and Kostrikin.

Adyan asked, "You say that with your method, Freiman solved the problem? What is the essence of your method?"

"I studied directly the structure of the set of sums of continued fractions and avoided Hall's lemmas, which, as Bumby showed, were exhausted."

"But the avoidance of Hall's lemmas is not a method. Why did you not find the source of the ray with your methods?"

"That is a difficult task. It required several years to solve it."

Kostrikin started to speak of the computational part of the dissertation. He implied that the calculations were not to be trusted. And then an ominous phrase hung in the air (then attached to the report). "In your work the mathematics is merely mechanical."

Summing up, Andrianov said: "The work is put together badly, that is clear." And he noisily slapped a copy of the dissertation as if to bury it. Meanwhile from the other side of the door Adyan could be heard saying, "Make a note that it has no theoretical value."

The whole discussion lasted about ten minutes.

The story is so typical and striking that it is worth repeating.

## On the Nationality of the Authors of Dissertations caught on the hook of the Expert Committee

On 6 December 1976 the following people were summoned by the Expert Committee:

1. Krivoshei, Efim Shlomovich
2. Shneiberg, Iosif Yakovlevich
3. Bershtein, Aleksandr Azriil'evich
4. Kropp, Leonid Efimovich
5. Frenkin, Boris Rafailovich
6. Mogilevskii, Mikhail Grigor'evich

A total of six people—all six of them were Jewish.

At the meeting of the committee during which the work of Shnepperman, Tsalenko and Rozenberg was discussed, eleven people were summoned to appear. All eleven of them were Jewish.

Here is a discussion in which I have used extracts from documents relating to the dissertation of Boris Moiseevich Shain, which was rejected in 1969, the first in a series of rejections of Jewish dissertation.

Vagner: (Doctor of Sciences, specialist on semigroups, and a teacher of Shain): "The dissertation is a fundamental piece of research, of an unusual richness of content, which contains a large quantity of major results. This important scientific work is a valuable contribution to modern algebra and establishes its author as a talented scientist."

Expert Committee (Their decision): "In the dissertation there are no important scientific results that merit the degree of Doctor of

Sciences. The dissertation contains a large number of uninteresting theorems and extremely cumbersome formulations."

Kurosh (Head of the Soviet school of general algebra, from the report which I reproduced from memory): "The dissertation is a substantial contribution to science. The Expert Committee was not guided by a strong desire to get at the truth and this is a reflection of a lowering in the moral standards of a significant number of Soviet mathematicians. The work was sent to be read by mathematicians who should have refused to give a report on the grounds of their lack of competence to do so. As a result of the attitude manifested by the committee in this case, I would find further work on the committee very difficult."

Gluskin (Doctor of Sciences, specialist in the theory of semigroups): "The decision taken by the Expert Committee to reject the dissertation has surprised everyone who is at all familiar with the work. I cannot agree with that decision. I believe it is absolutely mistaken."

Adyan (From the stenographic reports of the meeting of the Expert Committee, held in the absence of the defendant): "He has about a hundred works to his name. He must be chasing after recognition."
  Il'in: "But perhaps his results will become well-known?"
  Yablonskii: "I am struck by his views on the application of his results."
  Gnedenko: "It is a difficult case. He is a capable mathematician, and he will be difficult to handle."
  Adyan: "He is extremely capable. I agree with Kurosh. He is a brilliant mathematician, but superficial."
  Unknown: "It is already late. Let us make a decision. We are not getting to the point."
  Il'in: "If there is more than one negative opinion we must take a vote. What does the group propose?"
  Adyan: "Reject it."
  Unknown: "But we must formulate the conclusions of the committee. Who will draw them up?"

Unknown: "Let whoever abstains draw them up."

Adyan: "We will draw them up."

Kostrikin: "We must include that we have some doubts, or perhaps we should just write that we are not able to reach a positive decision."

Il'in: "But we are the experts, and you two are the specialists. The plenum will only send back our report for reconsideration."[8]

I cannot help adding a comment here. Note that all of them know that they must reject a talented work. They knew that beforehand, although the stenographic records offer no proof of that assumption. The only thing they did not know was how to justify their rejection. Compare this with the opinion of the specialists.

Gluskin: "The words of the Expert Committee regarding the absence of significant results in the work can only be based on complete ignorance of the dissertation. This is not merely my own opinion. The results are highly regarded by all Soviet specialists in the field, and I could also introduce here the opinion of foreign specialists. In 1967, in the United States, the second volume of a monograph by the prominent specialists Clifford and Preston, *Algebraic Theory of Semigroups*, appeared that summarizes the developments of the last decade. In this book the results of the dissertation (the authors call it the 'Shain theory') are given great prominence. The editors of a new international journal *Semigroups* (to which the leading specialists in the field contribute) decided to open the first issue of the journal with a large review article by Shain."

*Kostrikin* (from the minutes): "We shall ask you a series of questions. Have you read the report of Anatolii Illarionovich Shirshov?"

*Shain*: "I should like to reply to the criticism of all three of the readers."

*Kostrikin*: "No, reply to the last report."

*Shain*: "Very well. The reader is convinced that the standard

8. Again I would like to draw the reader's attention to the fact that this conversation is not the author's creation. It is taken from the stenographic reports of the meeting, and every word is genuine.

concepts of the theory of semigroups were first introduced by me. That shows how much the reader is acquainted with semigroups. He comes out in essence against the whole theory of semigroups since he does not distinguish between that which I have done and that which was already known. . . . The typist played a nasty trick on the reader, when she made a small typing error in one of the references of my dissertation. He writes of a mythical theorem of Keisler, and then makes the comment that it is very well known. That in itself speaks volumes about. . . ."

*Gonchar*: "But the theory is well known?"

*Shain*: "To the specialist—yes."

*Gonchar*: "Then that is why the reader called the theorem famous."

*Shain*: "Pardon me. If the theorem were well known to the reader, he would not have called it Keisler's theorem."

*Adyan*: "But the reader took you at your word. In your dissertation there is a typing error and that is why the reader speaks of Keisler's theorem."

*Shain*: "But why does he then refer to it as 'well known'?"

*Adyan*: "You yourself allowed a typing error to pass and now you blame the reader."

*Shain*: "I am not accusing the reader of making a typing error. He called something well known with which he is not at all familiar. That tells us something about the value of his opinions. By the way, if that example is not enough I can give you several more of the same kind."

*Me*: "What an expressive scene! The respected reader has been caught red-handed. His ignorance and his trickery have been exposed. The members of the committee rush in to save him but they cannot brush it all to one side, so they pretend they have not heard. Look how Shain was diverted from this delicate subject, and was addressed for the first and last time politely by his name and patronymic, as verified in the minutes."

*Shain*: "Perhaps that is not enough. All right, here is another fact."

*Kostrikin*: "Boris Moiseevich, a doctoral dissertation in mathematics should be intelligible to every mathematician. . . ."

Whew! what hard work. It was like trying to drown a hippopotamus in a swamp.

## Miscellaneous

Mathematicians whose doctoral dissertations have been rejected by the Expert Committee at VAK include: Markus, Shain, Shnepperman, Zhmud', Levin, Shmul'yan, Mil'man, Norkin, Balk, Tsalenko, Vinberg, Lekhtman, Pekelis. And the list is far from complete.

Rubinov's doctoral dissertation has been with VAK for over six years. This example is typical and such lengths of time have become quite usual.

Lozanovskii's doctoral dissertation lay in a file at VAK for several years. He died. A few months later the degree was confirmed.

When Tsalenko defended his doctoral dissertation at Moscow University, the results were: 31 for, 1 against. When he defended it a second time at the Steklov Institute the results were 10 against, and 1 abstention.

Arnol'd and Fomenko were removed from the meeting of the Academic Council during the second defense of Vinberg's doctoral dissertation. Academician Mardzhanishvili flung open the doors for them with his own hand.

The mathematician L asked his friend V, a worker at the Steklovka:
  "Will you be a reader at my doctoral defense?"
  "Under no circumstances," he replied. "I would lose my job."

Frenkin's dissertation was approved. L, a mathematical physicist, remarked so that all could hear at the meeting of the Expert Committee, "He is my wife's graduate student."
  All the mathematical physicists voted to confirm the work, and all the mathematicians abstained. Don't forget we are talking about a work of mathematics.

The Expert Committee decided to reject Roitman's dissertation on the grounds that the Academic Council of Kalinin State University had conducted the defense after its period of authority had expired.

It is very strange that they could not find the document that prolonged the authority of the council, although many people said there was such a document.

It is also strange that the Expert Committee should concern itself with the administrative aspect of the case to the detriment of the scientific aspect.

It is also strange that after Roitman's defense, the same Academic Council considered the dissertations of three other people and they were all confirmed by VAK without delay.

But VAK rejected Roitman's work.

During the discussions of the reappointment of Professor Shilov to Moscow State University, he was abused for employing too many Jews who might leave the country. One of the speakers said that Shilov's reply to the criticism was not sufficiently anti-Semitic. "No . . . no . . . ," he corrected himself, "I meant anti-Zionist." We don't need Freud to understand the meaning of that slip of the tongue.

The reelection was put off to the following year.

The next day Shilov was walking by the university with his wife, when he suddenly felt ill. He sat down on the step at the entrance to the university clinic and his wife ran upstairs for the doctor. The doctor refused to come down and insisted that the sick man come in himself. While they were arguing, Shilov died.

### And Where Am I?

I am writing these concluding lines a year later, in the spring of 1978.

Last autumn in Dushanbe a conference was held on number theory, at which its organizers could say with satisfaction: "For the first time—*Judenfrei!*"

I did not even get an answer to my letter asking to participate, never mind an invitation.

In the autumn I wrote to academician Bogolyubov that all was not well with Soviet mathematics.

Bogolyubov did not answer.

Recently I tried to see the president of the Academy, but to no avail. Even his assistant would not see me.

I must publish my notes.

"But where am I?"

Karatsuba knows perfectly well.

At the end of the Vilnius conference on number theory there was a banquet where, after several toasts to Lithuanian and Russian mathematicians, a toast was proposed to all Soviet mathematicians.

"Fine," Karatsuba said for all to hear, "but without the Yids."

The hero of a Polish joke goes home to find the lodger in bed with his wife. He looks around at the unbearably cramped conditions in his room and asks himself, "And where am I?"

And he answers, "Standing in line for carp."

I do not want to stand in line for carp. Over and over, not finding the answer, I ask myself the same question:

"And where am I?"

# Appendix A
The Situation in Soviet Mathematics

# Appendix B
"Jewish Problems" in Mathematics

# Appendix C
Remarks on "'Jewish Problems' in Mathematics"

# Appendix A

## The Situation in Soviet Mathematics
## By Emigré Soviet Mathematicians

## 1. A little history

Before World War II the situation in Soviet mathematics was better than in other fields. Ideological pressure in mathematics was less severe than in the humanities, biology, and even physics, where relativity theory was denounced as idealistic (this occurred at Moscow University). The general policy of discrimination against the old intelligentsia was felt in mathematics too: there were restrictions on access to education for children from nonproletarian families and for children of the so-called enemies of the people. But the consequences of this policy were softened by the influence of prominent scholars, who often managed to persuade the authorities to make exceptions for the most talented young people. Even the purges of the thirties, which drained many areas of Russian culture, left mathematics almost intact. (N. N. Luzin was hounded in the press, but he was not arrested and remained an academician.)

A new development in Soviet life at the end of World War II was official anti-Semitism. It first affected mathematicians in 1944–45, when the Ministry of Higher Education began discriminating against Jewish applicants for admission to graduate schools. Soon party organizations at universities started objecting to graduate students with Jewish last names. The discrimination was never open. It was carried out under various pretexts: insufficient participation in political activities, low grades in political disciplines, and the like. It was considered slanderous to talk about anti-Semitic tendencies; students who did so were harassed to the point of expulsion from the university.

Although the existence of anti-Semitism could not be discussed, it was possible to fight for individual cases. In the first years after the war, mathematicians did their best to defend Jewish students and often succeeded. Particular mention should be made of the great roles played in this regard by V. V. Stepanov, then director of the Mathematical Institute at Moscow University, and by I. G. Petrovskii, first dean and later rector of Moscow University. In Leningrad, V. I. Smirnov fought passionately against injustice. Nevertheless, discrimination gradually spread to university admissions, to job placement after graduation, and so on.

The elimination of Jews from the scientific institutions began. The most dramatic events occurred in the Ukraine in the late 1940s, when almost all Jewish scientists were forced out of the Kiev Mathematical Institute—including B. Korenblum, M. Krasnoselsky, M. Krein, and S. Krein—and the Functional Analysis Seminar was dismantled.

In the last years of Stalin's life, anti-Semitism in Russia became hysterical. In Khrushchev's era the situation improved, but anti-Jewish discrimination did not stop completely and the publicly condemned list of Stalin's excesses did not include anti-Semitism.

In the beginning of the sixties, the moral atmosphere in mathematics worsened noticeably. Positions of influence were seized by mathematicians who carried through anti-Semitic policies with great zeal and enthusiasm. Their activities permitted the spread of anti-Semitism into areas where purely bureaucratic control is insufficient and where the implementation of anti-Semitic policies requires acts of collusion by qualified mathematicians. Such areas include the publication of books and articles and the awarding of degrees.

## 2. The role of the Academy of Sciences

The Academy of Sciences occupies a special position in the USSR as the monitor of all scientific activities, including the publication of results, contacts with foreign scientists, the work assignment of top level scientists, and so on. Until the late fifties, only mathematicians of great scientific stature were elected Members and Corresponding Members of the Academy. Then the situation changed radically. When the Siberian division of the Academy was opened, numerous middle-level scientists were elected to the Academy because of their invitation to work in Siberia. At approximately the same time, the government announced a number of vacancies for applied mathematicians involved in classified research. These vacancies were filled by people absolutely unknown in the mathematical world. As a result, the scientific level of the mathematical division of the Academy fell significantly. A stable majority formed which, interested in preserving the new status, has rejected many deserving candidates. Distinguished mathematicians like I. M. Gel'fand, M. G. Krein, S. P. Novikov, and I. R. Shafarevich were nominated many times for election as Academicians and rejected every time. (Gel'fand, Novikov, and Shafarevich are Corresponding Members of the Academy. Only Novikov was elected in the last decade. Gel'fand and Shafarevich were elected much earlier.) In the same way, V. I. Arnold, N. V. Efimov, O. A. Lady-zhenskaya, Yu. I. Manin, O. A. Oleinik, Ya. G. Sinai, M. I. Vishik, and other internationally recognized mathematicians were voted down as Corresponding Members.

The Steklov Mathematical Institute is a prestigious institution in the field of mathematics. For the last thirty years its director has been academician I. M. Vinogradov, who is proud of the fact that under his leadership the Institute has become "free of Jews."

Unlike the situation in the first years after World War II, the key positions in mathematics nowadays are occupied by people who are not only unwilling to protect the interests of science and scientists in the face of the authorities, but who go even beyond official guidelines in their policies of political and racial discrimination. Not only Jews, but also other mathematicians disliked by the ruling group are given a hard time.

It is instructive to follow the evolution of L. S. Pontryagin. During the thirties and forties, Pontryagin was an outstanding scientist who expended considerable effort helping those of his pupils and colleagues who were persecuted for political or racial reasons. A change in personality brought out strong anti-Semitic tendencies. As a result, he was immediately promoted to important administrative positions: he has represented the USSR in the International Mathematical Union, he heads the editorial board that makes the final decision on books on mathematics proposed for publication to the publishing house *Nauka*, and following I. G. Petrovskii's death he was appointed editor of the oldest Soviet mathematical journal, *Matematicheskii Sbornik*.

The anti-Semitic activity of Vinogradov and Pontryagin is fully supported by Academy Members Vladimirov, Dorodnitsyn, and Tikhonov, who have perhaps less anti-Jewish prejudice, but find this policy profitable.

The National Committee of Soviet Mathematicians controls the international contacts of Soviet mathematicians. The committee determines the membership of delegations to international conferences and has to approve all the lectures by Soviet mathematicians. The leading nucleus of the committee does its best to prevent trips abroad by scientists who happen to be Jewish, even when the trip is recommended by the employing institution and by the local party organization.

Before the creation of the National Committee in the late sixties, no organized attempts had been made to influence invitations of Soviet mathematicians to international congresses. The authorities simply did not grant exit visas to individuals who were not in their favor, but it was possible to send manuscripts of lectures by mail. Even before the Nice Congress of 1970, however, S. V. Yablonskii, representing the National Committee, tried to exclude some Jews from the list of the invited speakers. He did not succeed in the attempt, but in revenge the committee did drop from the Russian edition of the proceedings the lectures it had not approved. Before the next Congress (Vancouver, 1974) new tactics were employed. The following letter, signed by Vinogradov, was sent to a number of institutes. "The National Committee has discussed the invitation of the member of your staff _____ to the International Congress of Mathematicians and has decided not to include him in the Soviet delegation. We do not recommend sending _____'s manuscript to the Congress."

The people targeted by these letters included Arnol'd, Dobrushin, Dynkin, Kazhdan, Henkin, and others. Only in two cases did the heads of the institutes refuse to obey Vinogradov and send the addresses (but of course not the speakers!).

Famous names like Vinogradov and Pontryagin are of special value to Soviet anti-Semites, but most discrimination is carried out by mathematicians of the next generation. One must mention in this regard S. V. Yablonskii, corresponding member of the Academy of Sciences, E. F. Mishchenko, deputy director of the Steklov Institute, S. B. Stechkin, editor of the journal *Matematicheskie Zametki*, V. I. Il'in and P. L. Ul'yanov, professors at Moscow University, and Yu. L. Ershov and B. A. Rogosin, professors at Novosibirsk University and Novosibirsk Institute of Mathematics.

## 3. The publication of scientific works

Discrimination in this area dates from the last decade, and Pontryagin has played an outstanding role in this respect. A striking example is the history of *Matematicheski Sbornik*.

The editorial board before February 1975 consisted of the following: I. G. Petrovskii (editor), P. S. Aleksandrov, K. I. Babenko, N. V. Efimov, A. A. Gonchar, M. V. Keldysh, A. A. Kirillov, A. N. Kolmogorov, Yu. I. Manin, V. A. Marchenko, K. K. Mardzhanishvili, M. M. Postnikov, L. A. Skornyakov, M. I. Vishik. Now the new editorial board consists of: L. S. Pontryagin (editor), P. S. Aleksandrov, A. N. Andrianov, V. A. Andrunakievich, A. A. Gonchar, K. K. Mardzhanishvilii, V. P. Mikhailov, E. G. Poznyak, A. A. Samarskii, P. L. Ul'yanov, S. V. Yablonskii. The change in editorial policy can be traced in Table A.

## Table A

| Year | 1970 | | | 1971 | | | 1972 | | | 1973 | | | 1974 | | |
|---|---|---|---|---|---|---|---|---|---|---|---|---|---|---|---|
| Volume | 81 | 82 | 83 | 84 | 85 | 86 | 87 | 88 | 89 | 90 | 91 | 92 | 93 | 94 | 95 |
| Total number of articles | 34 | 38 | 36 | 34 | 37 | 33 | 36 | 37 | 36 | 36 | 32 | 38 | 37 | 43 | 31 |
| Number of articles of Jewish authors | 11 | 20 | 12 | 17 | 15 | 16 | 14 | 10 | 9 | 11 | 11 | 12 | 11 | 12 | 10 |

| Year | 1975 | | | 1976 | | | 1977 | | | 1978 | | |
|---|---|---|---|---|---|---|---|---|---|---|---|---|
| Volume | 96 | 97 | 98 | 99 | 100 | 101 | 102 | 103 | 104 | 105 | 106 | 107 |
| Total number of articles | 33 | 29 | 34 | 34 | 37 | 30 | 34 | 32 | 29 | 30 | 34 | 30 |
| Number of articles of Jewish authors | 7 | 2 | 3 | 3 | 2 | 3 | 4 | 1 | 0 | 4 | 2 | 4 |

# Appendix A

In *Soviet Mathematics—Doklady* all articles are transmitted by academicians. After radical changes in the membership of the Academy many important results, especially by young authors, do not reach the *Doklady*. A great part of them are published in the section of short communications of the *Uspekhi Matematicheskikh Nauk* labeled as the *Communications of the Moscow Mathematical Society*.

The section of physics and mathematics of the publishing house "Nauka" is the main publisher of mathematical monographs in the country. Before the end of the sixties, the fate of manuscripts depended mainly on their scientific level. Recently an editorial board was organized and headed by Pontryagin. Yablonskii is an active member. This has led to a radical change in the editorial policy. Manuscripts by Jews and other unwanted people are often rejected even when they are prepared on the initiative of the publisher.

The same policy is enforced in the preparation of the *Mathematical Encyclopedia*. Almost all proposals to invite contributions from Jewish authors are rejected by editors under different pretexts. The already-published volume one contains 346 articles and only 10 are written by authors with "dubious" last names. References to emigrants are prohibited. For example, I. Dolgachev was forbidden to mention the name of Pyatetskii-Shapiro in his paper on homogeneous domains or even to include Pyatetskii-Shapiro's book in the list of references. Because of this, Dolgachev refused to write the article.

The power of a small group (I. M. Vinogradov, L. S. Pontryagin, S. V. Yablonskii, A. A. Dorodnitsyn) was vividly illustrated when a collection of survey articles, *Mathematics in the USSR, 1958–1967*, was being prepared. Before the preparation of this collection, surveys covering the period 1917–57 had been published under the auspices of the Moscow Mathematical Society. This new volume was prepared and edited by G. E. Shilov and S. V. Fomin. A few dozen of the most competent specialists prepared articles surveying all fields of mathematics. Many more mathematicians were involved in collecting materials and writing separate sections of the articles. The surveys were approved by the Council of the Moscow Mathematical Society and by the publishing house. However, only the second volume (the bibliographies) appeared. The material composed for the first volume (the survey articles) was destroyed by a decision of a committee headed by Dorodnitsyn. It never was published in spite of a letter from Petrovskii, the rector of Moscow University, and in spite of the resolution passed at a meeting of the Moscow Mathematical Society. The work of dozens of mathematicians was wasted.

## 4. Admission to institutions of higher learning

The discrimination against Jewish young people began in the Ukraine. In 1948, for example, one-third to one-half of the student body of the Odessa Institute of Telecommunication was Jewish. In 1952, Jews made up only 4 percent of the new admissions. Hardly any Jews were admitted to the department of physics of Moscow University and to the Moscow Institute of Engineering Physics. Before the middle of the sixties, however, discrimination in admission to the Faculty of Mechanics and Mathematics of Moscow University occurred only occasionally. In view of the exceptional role of Moscow University in the preparation of mathematical scientists, the policy used in the admission to the Faculty is not a local issue but is of national importance. Among the students admitted in 1964, 84 out of 410 were identified as Jews in their passports. (The domestic passports of Soviet citizens mention their ethnic nationality. In the case of different nationalities of father and mother, the nationality of the child may be chosen by the parents.) The discrimination increased dramatically in 1968 and reached its present form in 1970: Since then only 2 to 4 Jews among 400 to 500 students are admitted each year. They are mostly relatives or friends of influential people. Among the rejected are many winners of Mathematical Olympiads, i.e., individuals who manifest great mathematical capability. Some discrimination is also directed against non-Jews of the "intelligentsia," in particular, graduates of some special mathematical high schools with the reputation as "breeding-grounds of liberalism."

Effective methods for implementing the discrimination have been devised. More or less independent professors are excluded from giving entrance examinations. The written test consists of two rather simple problems and two or three problems requiring cumbersome calculations and the examination of many particular cases. The time is strictly limited and only solutions without any minor slips are given credit. As a result, mediocre students who solve only two simple problems get the same grades as the best students who practically solve the rest of the problems as well, but are penalized for minimal inaccuracies. In this way the bright students are deprived of their advantage on the only exam that might be evaluated by objective criteria.

On orals in mathematics and physics, specially selected examiners give Jews very difficult problems requiring knowledge beyond the high-school program and allow a very short time for answers. A. A. Karatsuba is known as one of the creators of the special problems for Jews and as a person who coaches the examiners. For those who survive this treatment, there remains the written test in Russian composition and a gifted young mathematician is given a failing grade for "insufficiently developed theme." Among the heads of examinations committees in recent years, P. L. Ul'yanov, B. V. Gnedenko, A. A. Gonchar and E. M. Nikishin are well remembered.

For some years gifted young mathematicians turned down by Moscow University entered the division of applied mathematics of two Moscow schools: the Institute of Electronics and the Institute of Transportation. Both Institutes accepted extremely strong classes. A few years ago, however, the Institute of Electronics stopped accepting Jews almost completely, and in 1977 the Institute of Transportation did the same.

## 5. Dissertations and degrees

There exist in the Soviet Union two advanced academic degrees. The "Candidate of Sciences" degree corresponds approximately to an American Ph.D.; "Doctor of Sciences" is a much higher degree and less than one of ten Candidates reaches it.

Up until the late sixties, good Doctor of Sciences dissertations were accepted for defense without any discrimination. The defense was usually successful and the degrees were quickly confirmed by the expert committees of VAK (the Higher Certification Commission).

At the end of the sixties, difficulties began with VAK's confirmation of doctoral dissertations. At that time G. E. Shilov resigned in protest from VAK. Doctoral dissertations by Jews, especially in algebra, theory of functions, functional analysis, and cybernetics, were sent out for additional review to specially selected readers. This caused the review process to last six years or more, and in most cases resulted in a refusal. More recently, this arbitrariness has also been applied to non-Jewish candidates who either have Jewish advisors or are simply out of favor with the members of VAK.

Among doctoral dissertations turned down by VAK are those of Balk, Belitsky, Brudny, Vinberg, Markus, Tsalenko, and Shmulyan. The majority of "undesirable" mathematicians, however, simply cannot find a place to submit their dissertations or, knowing the reality, do not even try. Therefore, many world renowned mathematicians have no doctoral degree. At the same time, the doctoral degree is awarded without any delay to persons unknown for their achievements in science but having a different kind of merit. One of the newest Doctors of Sciences is Sadovnichy, who excelled during his tenure as assistant dean in 1970–75 in perfecting the present system of admission to the Faculty of Mechanics and Mathematics at Moscow University.

Until about 1970–72 no great difficulties arose with the Candidate of Sciences dissertations. Now the situation has changed. As in the case of doctoral degrees, there are three stages: acceptance of a dissertation by an institution, the defense, and the confirmation by VAK. The main discrimination, which is almost invisible to the public, is applied at the first stage. In the last five years the academic institutions of Moscow and Leningrad almost stopped accepting dissertations from Jews. But for some time it was possible to find a place in other cities to defend dissertations. A few years ago, however, VAK was reorganized, and the right of awarding degrees in each field of mathematics was left to only a small number of institutions. Many outstanding scientists were excluded from degree-awarding councils and their places were taken by individuals known more for their political than scientific activity.

As a result, even if a dissertation by a Jewish student is admitted for a defense, it is often turned down despite the fact that all participants in the discussion testify to the high quality of the work. Such incidents have become more and more common at Moscow University over the last few years. A striking example is the defense of Gutkin on October 15, 1976. Even a successful defense is not always confirmed by VAK.

The main responsibility for the present practices of VAK lies with A. N. Tikhonov, V. A. Il'in (the former chairman of the expert committee in mathematics), V. S. Vladimirov (the present chairman), A. A. Gonchar (a deputy chairman), P. L. Ul'yanov, S. B. Stechkin, V. M. Millionshchikov, and S.V. Yablonskii.

## 6. What western mathematicians can do

It is possible to hold varying political views. One may believe that the structure of Soviet society is the concern of the Soviet people. But whatever one's political views, it should be possible to distinguish between honesty and dishonesty and to uphold a universal standard of professional ethics. It is crucial that the world mathematical community be aware of the unprincipled behavior of certain groups of influential mathematicians in the Soviet Union and that these mathematicians feel the moral disapproval of their colleagues. Within the Soviet Union, there is no way for public opinion to express itself. It is therefore all the more

94

## Appendix A

important that each arbitrary action receive an adequate response outside the Soviet Union.

Much too often in the Soviet Union, foreign travel is simply a reward for political services. (The only one to benefit from such a trip is the traveler himself, and his benefits are primarily material.) It is necessary to insist that real scholars be included in scientific exchange programs. If the world mathematical community is willing to persevere, this goal can be achieved. Otherwise, scientific exchange makes no sense.

One should not be afraid that publicity may hurt Soviet mathematicians. Experience shows that publicity is in fact their best protection against arbitrariness.

An invitation sent to a Soviet scholar is important even when it cannot be accepted. Given the present conditions in Soviet mathematics, recognition abroad is the only way to distinguish truly scientific achievements from reputations gained through political machinations.

In view of the difficulties involved in publishing good works in the Soviet Union, it would be useful to send more invitations to Soviet scholars asking them to send their articles and those of their pupils to western journals. In spite of bureaucratic red tape, publication in the west of articles and even of books is sometimes possible.

ALTHOUGH THE AUTHORS of the report, "The Situation in Soviet Mathematics," are now outside the Soviet Union, revealing their names could do harm to persons in the USSR connected with them. We believe that the authors have made every effort to present a true picture of the situation.

MICHAEL ARTIN, *Massachusetts Institute of Technology*
HYMAN BASS, *Columbia University*
ISRAEL N. HERSTEIN, *University of Chicago*
MELVIN HOCHSTER, *University of Michigan*
NATHAN JACOBSON, *Yale University*
MARK KAC, *Rockefeller University*
JACK C. KIEFER, *University of California at Berkeley*
JOSEPH J. KOHN, *Princeton University*
RICHARD S. PALAIS, *Brandeis University*
ALEX ROSENBERG, *Cornell University*
IRVING E. SEGAL, *Massachusetts Institute of Technology*
ALLEN L. SHIELDS, *University of Michigan*
ISADORE M. SINGER, *University of California at Berkeley*
DONALD C. SPENCER, *Princeton University*
ELIAS M. STEIN, *Princeton University*

# Appendix B

## "Jewish Problems" in Mathematics
## By *Melvyn B. Nathanson*

To enter *Mekhmat*, the Faculty of Mechanics and Mathematics of Moscow State University, a student must take four examinations: written and oral examinations in mathematics, an oral examination in physics, and a written examination in Russian composition. The admissions procedure has been distorted to exclude Jewish students. At the oral mathematics examination, the student draws by lot a ticket with two questions. After he answers these questions, the examiner asks him several more questions. For Jewish applicants, there are special problems, called "Jewish problems," whose solution requires knowledge far beyond that contained in the secondary school curriculum in the USSR. The problems are often difficult variants of those given in the Moscow Mathematical Olympiad or the International Mathematical Olympiad. In the Olympiads, students have about one hour to solve each problem. The oral examiners for *Mekhmat* give a student only from ten to twenty minutes. Even when a particularly brilliant student manages to solve some of these "Jewish problems," he still gets a failing grade. There is no hope.

Below is a list of special "Jewish problems" used in the oral examination for *Mekhmat* in 1978:

1. Which is larger: $\sqrt[4]{413}$ or $6 + \sqrt[3]{3}$?

2. Solve the equation $x^y = y^x$ in positive integers.

3. Prove that a convex polygon of area 1 contains a triangle of area 1/4.

4. Show that the following statement is false:
   A convex polyhedron of volume 1 contains a tetrahedron of volume 1/8.

   A natural estimate is not $(1/2)^3 = 1/8$ but $(1/3)^3 = 1/27$. Obtain this estimate and try to improve it.

5. Does there exist an infinite family of pairwise noncongruent right triangles such that the lengths of the sides are natural numbers and the lengths of the two short sides differ by 1?

## Appendix B

6. A function of two variables $f(x,y)$ takes on at least 3 values. For some fixed numbers $a$ and $b$ we have $f(a,y) \neq$ constant and $f(x,b) \neq$ constant. Prove that there exist numbers $p$, $q$, $r$, $s$ such that $f(p,q)$, $f(r,q)$, $f(p,s)$ are three pairwise-distinct values of the function $f(x,y)$.

7. Let $ABC$ be a triangle. Construct a straight line that divides into two equal parts both its area and its perimeter.

8. Let $ab = 4$ and $c^2 + 4d^2 = 4$. Prove the inequality $(a - c)^2 + (b - d)^2 \geq 1.6$.

9. Prove the inequality $((\sin x)/x)^3 \geq \cos x$ for $x \in (0, \pi/2]$.

10. Prove the inequality $(\sin x)^{-2} \geq x^{-2} + 1 - (4/\pi^2)$ for $x \in (0, \pi/2]$.

11. Let $ABCDE$ be a convex pentagon with the property that each of the five triangles $ABC$, $BCD$, $CDE$, $DEA$, and $EAB$ has area 1. Find the area of the pentagon $ABCDE$.

12. Solve the following equation in rational numbers:
$(x + y\sqrt{2})^2 + (z + t\sqrt{2})^2 = 5 + 4\sqrt{2}$.

13. On the edges of a tetrahedron of volume 1 there are given 6 points, none of which are vertices. Consider the four tetrahedrons constructed as follows: Choose one vertex of the original tetrahedron and let the remaining vertices be the three points given on the three edges incident to the chosen vertex. Prove that at least one of these four tetrahedrons has volume not exceeding 1/8.

# Appendix C

## Remarks on "'Jewish Problems' in Mathematics"
## By *Andrei Sakharov*
## Translated by Melvyn B. Nathanson

These problems affect me deeply. I believe that to give such problems on an entrance examination is absolutely intolerable. The problems are exceedingly complicated and require extraordinary concentration and precision in carrying out lengthy computations. They presuppose knowledge and experience that far exceed what even the most gifted student could possibly possess. It is particularly inexcusable to give these problems on the *oral* examination, where the student is in a tense psychological situation and has only twenty minutes to find a solution.

I chose one of the problems on the list. Of course, the student taking the examination is not allowed to choose the particular problem he wishes to solve. I found a very pretty solution to my problem, but it required a nontrivial and ingenious argument, and it took me much more than one hour. Moreover, I was able to work quietly at home. I needed to use my considerable experience in solving these difficult mathematical problems as well as my large store of mathematical knowledge. I tried to imagine the feelings of a boy or girl who comes to take this examination, on which his future depends, who gets such a problem, and who must try to solve it while sitting directly across from him an openly hostile examiner glances impatiently at his watch. The student must feel the evil and the cruelty in an examination that has been designed to destroy him, and we, too, cannot avoid the same feeling.

Compare the problems on this list with the problems given to other applicants who are not being discriminated against. The prejudice of the examiners is obvious.

This organized discrimination on the entrance examinations is used not only against Jews, but also against others, in particular, the children of dissidents. Moreover, to be admitted to Moscow State University, students who are not residents of Moscow must obtain a higher score on the entrance examinations than Moscow residents, and this is another form of discrimination.

12 June 1979